D1331771

LIFE TWO

HOW TO GET TO AND ENJOY
WHAT USED TO BE CALLED RETIREMENT

BY DON EZRA

Life Two
How To Get To And Enjoy What Used To Be Called Retirement
Copyright © 2019 by Don Ezra Consulting Services, Ltd.
All rights reserved.

ISBN: 978-0-9937339-2-5 Paperback
ISBN: 978-0-9937339-3-2 Electronic book

THIS BOOK IS DEDICATED TO
RICHARD, CLIVE, GORDON AND ZACK

Thanks for all those conversations and
comments, and the resulting
perspectives and insights
– and for your friendship

CONTENTS

PREFACE

Y OU'RE SHORT OF TIME. I get it. That's my problem. Your problem is that you occasionally think about retirement, and it's too complicated and you don't know where to start, so you avoid it. Or worse, it scares you – and again, you avoid it. My problem is to convince you, in a few minutes, that it shouldn't be scary or complicated, if you think about it logically. So I'll show you the logic, and how you can use it to create a plan for yourself that will ... well, I won't say it'll take care of everything, because that's just not credible. But it will at least put you in the driver's seat, so you can decide on your own direction and speed.

OK? You'll give me a few minutes? Here goes.

I'll spell out the retirement problem, outline the solution, and show you the benefits.

***

The problem. I'll try not to refer to it as retirement. That's an outdated word. It's really (l)ife (a)fter (f)ull-(t)ime (wo)rk. And when I wrote it that way, the acronym LAFTWO presented itself. And that sounds like Life Two. And suddenly all kinds of thoughts were triggered, and a framework presented itself. Life One, our grown-up life, is something we enter after an education that prepares us for it. My point is that we need an education for Life Two.

We hear, over and over again, that people don't start thinking about it until they're at least 50. Then the regret starts. "Oh gosh, I wish I'd done something about this earlier, when there was still lots of time." That's *regret*.

Anxiety starts a few years later. It becomes a huge concern, to the extent that it has negative effects on health and on workplace productivity – studies, journal articles, around the world, all testify to this.

It's not just: "I don't think I have a lot. Will I outlive my assets?" That's the financial angle. Which is, as it happens, the single biggest fear that people have as they approach Life Two – again, tons of evidence, around the world.

But there are psychological issues too: "Will I lose my identity?" Many of us are so used to our work that that's how we define ourselves, particularly if we're successful or enjoy our work – and so, when it stops, for some of us the identity question arises. We probably spend more time awake at work than we do at home. It's understandable if the workplace defines us. What's going to give us motivation and purpose in Life Two, making us feel valuable and worthwhile?

And there are practical issues: "How will I spend my time?" One big-name academic emailed me. He said his mother told him: "Don't retire. The idleness is unbearable." It's all very well saying we'll have a lot more free time. What if we don't want it because we don't know what to do with it? An extended vacation is great; a permanent vacation – thank you, but no.

Does any of that sound familiar?

***

Now the solution.

Education. In the form of this book and the accompanying website (https://donezra.com), which has been going for a while. And in the form of a guided tour of the land of Life Two, with me as your tour guide.

In the book we'll take it slowly. I call it the Walking Tour. I've identified the essential elements. We'll take them in stages. That's where you'll learn the principles involved. The walk will give you a framework, to understand how things work. Think of it as showing you the cover on the jig-saw puzzle box. Once you see the whole picture, it helps when you come across a single piece or a group of pieces, to have an idea where they fit in.

But it's more than principles. The walking stages have a teach-yourself-by-doing exercise for you at the end, because the best way to get ideas to stay in your head is for you to apply them to your own situation. That has the added benefit of creating your own plan, as you go along.

The website gives you a lot more background and detail, if you'd like to add something to the principles. Specifically, it has three additional dimensions. The most important is the companion book, *Freedom, Time, Happiness* (or *FTH*, for short). In fact that's the book I originally planned, but my website readers gave me the impression some of it was deeper than they needed or wanted. That's why I developed the Walking Tour, an extract of the essential parts of *FTH* with exercises added to each Walk. Think of *FTH* as the hop-on-hop-off bus tour (the Hoho Bus Tour, as I now think of it!) whenever you feel inclined to explore the land of Life Two more fully. In fact, after most of the Walks I identify complementary stages on the Hoho Bus Tour, stages that are related to the territory covered by that Walk and expand your perspective.

In addition, the website gives you access to a series of podcasts made jointly with the Canadian consulting firm Common Wealth. And it also preserves the original blog posts that introduced parts of *FTH*, and continues as an ongoing discussion forum.

The Walking Tour covers all three angles I mentioned earlier: psychological, practical, financial.

Check out what we'll look at, in the Outline of the Walking Tour. See if the routes cover ground that you'd like to explore. That's the best way to see if this book is for you.

***

At what stage of Life One should you take the Walking Tour?

Again, originally I thought in grander terms. But I've discovered a couple of books that do the job very nicely if you're just starting out or if you're perhaps a little further along in Life One and are seeking peace of mind and happiness as the background for your day-to-day life. I'll recommend them to you as part of the exercises.

(I have no financial connection with either of the authors, if you're wondering. I just admire them.) Anyway, that freed me up to focus on telling you about getting to and enjoying Life Two, in all its aspects.

As a rough idea, I think you should start the financial education about twenty years before you plan to enter Life Two. Give yourself time to change anything that you may decide needs changing – though it's never too late to take action, as you can guess. Start the psychological and practical education five years before Life Two, though of course it won't hurt you to co-ordinate it with the financial education. It doesn't hurt to get rid of the bogey-man who scares you!

And that's important. It's true, transitioning to Life Two is potentially scary. We all think that way. You're not alone. This is normal. Once you understand that, the fear starts to go away. You just need to take the first step. And that's actually what you're doing, by taking the Walking Tour.

***

I said I'd tell you about the benefits.

If you do one walk a week, along with the accompanying exercise, you'll be amazed at how far you'll have come in less than six months.

You'll know yourself better, and what motivates you and makes you happy. You'll have identified activities to fill your time – and how to co-ordinate them with your partner. You'll have found out, along the way, about your government pension and taxation and healthcare and long-term care. You'll have an idea of your Life Two income, and how much of your life's essentials and your life's nice-to-haves it will support – and what you can do about it if your finances are still not where you'd like them to be.

So of course you'll know how to make the most use of a financial professional, if you look for one. And you'll be ready to talk to the next generation about your will and whatever other arrangements you'll have put into effect.

To the extent all of this isn't finished, you'll have made an explicit to-do list of the remaining items to complete.

Again, I can't say "Everything's going to be fine." But the Walking Tour should get rid of your *irrational* fears. Life Two won't be scary, any more. And for the rational fears, you'll know where you stand, you'll have a plan, you'll be in control of deciding direction and speed. You know that no plan will ever work out. But the work that's gone into the plan will help you adapt, as circumstances change – that's why we plan. And that gives you resilience.

My friends told me I should tell you something about myself, about how I've really been a popular teacher throughout my career, how I'm qualified by experience and research to talk about Life Two. They said it's a compelling story. No, not here – if that's of interest to you, you'll find it on the website. This is just the practical stuff here.

Thanks for the few minutes. I hope I've convinced you that it's worthwhile to take the Walking Tour. And by now you'll have an idea of my conversational teaching style.

Take the first step!

OVERVIEW OF THE WALKING TOUR

Walks 1-7 introduce you to Life Two.

Walks 8-10 are in the psychological/emotional neighborhood, for both yourself and your partner.

Walks 11-15 are in the financial neighborhood, and Walks 16-19 in the investment neighborhood.

Walks 20-21 bring it all together for your integrated financial plan for Life Two.

Walks 22-24 show you off as comfortable in Life Two, talking to others and celebrating.

A SPECIAL NOTE FOR COUPLES ON THE WALKING TOUR

SOME READERS ARE SINGLE, SOME of you are half of a couple. A friend suggests: "Is it worth saying a word about what happens if you have a partner?" Yes, thank you, that's a very good idea.

He adds: "I'm not trying to turn you into a marriage counselor, it just seems this is an issue you might want to touch on, especially if some of the exercises will require the participation of both." Yes; without giving any marriage guidance at all, I can identify some of the issues and Walks that are relevant for couples.

***

Start from the fact that, even if two of you are a couple and consider yourself a team, you and your partner are still two different people. So there are bound to be aspects of life that generate different views or different hopes and fears. In your time you've undoubtedly come across many such aspects, and you've found a way to cope with them, because here you are, together.

It's no different in Life Two. It's just that some aspects may be new, as they didn't come up or weren't important in Life One, but now they assume a greater importance. Let me identify some. They arise under all three of the main headings: psychological, practical, financial.

It may be useful for both of you to take Walk 2 ("What's useful for you?") so that you can identify where your differences lie, before you use other Walks to help you manage the identified aspects as a couple.

***

The psychological aspect is summed up in the question "Will I lose my identity?"

For some this will be a bigger issue than for the partner. It may be, for example, that one of the two of you identifies more closely with a role that will change in Life Two, or that one is more fearful of losing that sort of identity.

If both of you have this concern, it suggests to me that you can each offer empathetic support to the other, and remind yourselves that a very important identity – partner – isn't changing, so you start off on some firm ground.

If one has this concern and the other hasn't, I suggest that the more confident one should be understanding rather than impatient. "Don't be silly... Be sensible... Get on with your life..." These are likely to be less helpful and more divisive than recognizing that the concern is a common one, one that is not unnatural, and going on the Walks that attempt to help.

In particular, Walk 6 ("Is retirement complicated – or is it scary?"), Walk 7 ("Reinventing yourself in a new land") and Walk 8 ("Answering the deep question: who am I?") are relevant here.

Perhaps both of you might take these Walks and do the related Exercises, so that the more confident one will better understand what the more fearful partner is going through.

There's no right or wrong here – I'm just hoping these suggestions will be helpful in recognizing the scope of the issue in your case.

***

The practical aspect is summed up in the question "How will I spend my time?"

In a way, this is linked to the psychological question, because part of how you spend your time may be related to your identity or your mission or passion in life. And that's good. But there's a possible additional angle here, and it involves where you spend your time, because the location of your daily activities may well change in Life Two.

I think Walk 9 ("Answering the important question: what will I do?") and Walk 10 ("How healthy is your romantic Venn diagram?") are relevant here. And since the way you spend your time will involve both your relationship identities – remember you're an individual as well as part of a couple – it seems to me that you might both do the related exercises, or at least have the one who does them test the resulting proposed activities with the partner. This ought to help avoid or reduce situations where unexpected clashes might otherwise occur.

***

The financial aspect is summed up in the question "Will I outlive my assets?"

It's obviously a question that affects both you and your partner, since the assets are meant to provide for both of you. Or at least that's the assumption I make. If you have separate financial arrangements, then I'm guessing that the Walks apply to you as individuals rather than as a couple.

So the financial aspect really becomes an issue when only one partner (let's assume it's you) takes on the mantle of looking after the joint finances.

Many Walks involve information about both of you, but it isn't essential for both of you to be involved. For example, Walk 12 discusses your budget, Walk 14 discusses your Pillar 1 pensions, Walk 16 your assets, Walk 18 your extent of preparation for Life Two, Walks 20 and 21 your approach to accumulation and to decumulation (that is, drawing down amounts from your accumulated assets in order to generate cash for spending). All of these require collective information.

But all of that can be done by you, on your own. It's the Walks and Exercises involving attitudes and opinions – those are the ones that need to be considered together.

In the Exercise that follows Walk 12 (" A budget doesn't have to be detailed to be useful"), I ask you to split your budget between expenditures that you consider essential and expenditures on things that are nice to have. There's no right or wrong answer – and therefore identifying what's essential is best done as a joint exercise, in case one day you may have to abandon a "nice to have."

In the Exercise that follows Walk 13 ("How long should you plan to make your money last?"), you're essentially choosing a starting date for Life Two. Yes, that's best done with both of you in agreement!

In the Exercise that follows Walk 18 ("A first look at your projected Life Two income"), a fundamental question is whether you want your desired lifestyle to be supported by all your assets, or your liquid assets alone. For most of you, if you own a home, this essentially asks whether you want your home to be kept outside the assets that will generate spending money in Life Two. Again, that's a question to which agreement on the answer is desirable.

In the Exercise that follows Walk 19 ("Your risk choice depends on psychological and financial factors"), I ask you to consider how you'd react to cuts in your "nice to have" budget. This essentially completes the Exercise started after Walk 12. Again, both of you should agree on your attitudes, as this is fundamental to establishing what's your attitude to the risk that your desired lifestyle won't materialize in full. Incidentally, it's by no means a given that you'll agree. You're two different people, after all, and here's one area in which the difference may become apparent.

It's beyond the scope of the Walking Tour to show you the options you have if you find yourself in this situation. But you'll be glad to know that Stage I 33 on the Hoho Bus Tour explains the options in detail when partners have different attitudes towards risk.

***

Walk 23 deals with "Talking to your adult children about this phase of life." If you're going to lay out for your children the way you think about Life Two, including your financial position, it only makes sense for your partner to be involved in this conversation, whether as a prepared partner or as a recipient of information. If your partner survives you and you're the one with all the financial information, it will leave your partner much better off to know where everything is and what are the relevant financial consequences.

Walk 24, the final one, is just a celebration! Celebrate together!

ACQUAINT YOURSELF
WITH LIFE TWO

Walk 1

Raise A Glass To
The Peak Time
Of Life

WHERE THE ROUTE TAKES US

We'll start with an overview of Life Two, before the education actually gets going. And it's all good news. Far from being scary, Life Two is potentially the peak time of life. Prepare to be uplifted.

THE LEARNING

Three cheers for Life Two!

Hip-hip ... freedom! Hip-hip ... time! Hip-hip ... happiness!

Yes, Life Two is worth celebrating. It's potentially the most positive phase of life, the most enjoyable, the most rewarding.

***

Freedom? You can argue that freedom is never total, but we wouldn't want it to be. It's the limits in a civilized society that actually give us greater freedom to pursue what we want to do. Even libertarians stop at red lights, because they know that without traffic rules there would be chaos, and no scope to move forward with confidence.

Life Two reduces our obligations. It's in that sense that it gives us increased freedom. We ought to take advantage of the increased freedom. We've all dreamed of things we'd like to do. Life Two gives us the chance.

***

Time? We value it because of its scarcity while we're working. That's why, during our working careers, we look forward to weekends: fewer work obligations, more time for ourselves. Vacations are even better than weekends: quite simply, they're longer. And if you've been lucky enough to work in an environment that offers sabbaticals (as I was), that's best of all. People return from sabbaticals with stories of fulfillment, not just those who traveled or did something quite different from the daily routine of their lives; even those who decided to spend their time at home, undertaking a project or just plain relaxing, got satisfaction from finally being able to devote themselves to something they'd put off for lack of time.

Life Two increases the amount of time at our disposal.

***

Is it possible to have too much of a good thing? Too much freedom, too much time? Yes, of course it's possible, in a sense. Scarcity is one reason why we rate freedom and time so highly.

But also, we may not want more freedom and time. We may be so comfortable in our work routine that we don't want it to change. It may be (and for many, it really is) scary to contemplate any change. For many people, "retirement" is something that happens to them, or is done to them, and it takes them aback, it surprises and shocks them. Seeing it happen to someone else should be a wake-up call to us.

We should be ready for Life Two, just as we are for a vacation. We invariably see the positive side of vacations, and anticipate them eagerly, even if we enjoy our work. It should be the same with Life Two. We plan what we want to do on vacation. It should be the same with Life Two. Just a longer, more flexible vacation.

So I'll offer suggestions on how to think about the future, about who you are, about what you'll do, about the transition that most people go through, about how to make the most of Life Two.

**

Finances are always important. Money is one of two resources we have at our disposal, to convert into things that make us happy. That's why we accumulate it gradually during our working life, to be able to draw on it and convert it to freedom from work obligations. This is when we enjoy the reward for our financial sacrifices earlier in life.

The other spendable resource is, of course, time itself. We don't accumulate it; exactly the reverse – it's there, and it gradually expires, whether or not we use it – so it makes sense to use it while we have it.

Together, money and time are the ingredients for happiness – if we spend them well. So I'll include a Walk on how to spend time and money to enhance happiness.

**

Happiness? Yes, for many it's the ultimate goal on this earth.

Aristotle suggests that we choose happiness for its own sake and never as a means to something else, and that other things are important because they bring us happiness.

The fortunate thing is that our brain chemistry works automatically to make us happiest in this time of life. Did you know that? We actually enter Life Two with a built-in advantage! Studies in every country reveal the same pattern, over and over again. It's often called the U-curve of happiness. Let me explain it to you briefly – not that you need to be able to explain it to anyone else, but just for fun, as something you might care to tell someone at a party or barbecue or other gathering.

Happiness is typically high when we're young, it declines as we live our lives, and then it turns up again in the middle years of life, eventually surpassing the high level in our youth. The average age at which the curve turns upwards varies from country to country, but typically it bottoms out between 40 and 60. (Are you already wondering where you fit on this curve? People tell me it's their first thought!)

Of course, the big question is: why? And I think I've found an explanation. Here's the simplified version.

When we're young we lack experience. We know nothing! But we're going to change the world, right? In our youth, therefore, we seek knowledge and experience, through adventure. We seek excitement. Our anticipation is that adventure and excitement will bring happiness. We imagine how well things are going to turn out. "They lived happily ever after!" – that sort of feeling.

As we age and gain experience, we start to realize that few things work out as well as we expected or hoped. And we have the psychological and financial stresses of career advancement, and creating and raising a family. Of course many of these things bring happiness. But, as the saying goes, the devil is in the details. And it's the day-to-day stressful details, the complications we didn't expect, that reduce our happiness. At some stage we realize – and what triggers it varies from person to person, it varies in the intensity of the realization; for some people it's a cathartic mid-life crisis – but at some stage, we realize that life will never be perfect.

We recognize that perfection, achieving the ideal, as a goal is very difficult, because we can't anticipate the little things that don't go quite right. Instead of the idealist's "I'll accept nothing short of perfection!" we start to think: "Pretty good is ... pretty good! And it's enough!" We see the glass as half full rather than half empty.

Our measuring stick changes, as we age. It moves from idealistic standards (where everything falls short, and causes regret) to reality (where some things are pretty good). And then we find happiness in contentment, experiencing the things that are trusted and true. Another way to say this, is that we start to count our blessings.

There's a neurological explanation as to why this sort of thinking is essentially hard-wired into our brains – that's why the same pattern occurs everywhere. But for Walk 1, never mind that. Just smile as you think that, at any age, the best is yet to come!

DESTINATION

Put it all together: freedom, time, happiness. This is the BEST of life, for which the rest was made.

EXERCISE

There isn't one! Remember the saying that a journey of a thousand miles starts with a single step? Well, you've just taken the first step, and the journey is much, much shorter than that. Congratulations! Take it easy. See you again at the start of Walk 2.

COMPLEMENTARY STAGES ON THE HOHO BUS TOUR

You might enjoy Stage P1 in the Prologue (the portion of the Tour that contains a few thoughts before we start), reminding you why it's worth bothering at all, and Stage P2 in the Prologue, reminding you that retirement is a gift to ourselves. A different angle comes from Stage F 01 in Route 4 (exploring retirement finance), expanding on why it's worth saving, and Stage F 02 in

Route 4, on the huge multiplier effect of investing. Perhaps also Stage F 04 in Route 4, if you're still living in Life One, telling you about academic studies on the future (and happier) you.

Stage H 02 in Route 1 (exploring happiness and the psychology of Life Two) tells you more about why we feel happiest in our later years.

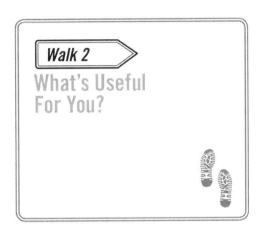

Walk 2

What's Useful
For You?

WHERE THE ROUTE TAKES US

In the Preface I mentioned three kinds of issues: psychological, practical, financial. You may have some of them or all of them. Let me explain how the Walking Tour is structured, so that you can see how you can best use it.

The learning

I've tried to create a question as a proxy for each of the three kinds of issues. So, check out the box below, and complete it by selecting one cell in each row. In this way you are saying, for each of the three kinds of issues, whether or not they bother you, and if they do, how much help you'd like in overcoming them.

	Not a problem for me	Do it for me	Do it with me	Help me do it myself
(Psychological) Will I lose my identity?				
(Practical) How will I spend my time?				
(Financial) Will I outlive my assets?				

If a question is not a problem for you, that's great. You can skip the Walks that deal with it, or, if you prefer, you can skim through them and see if there are any angles that are helpful even though it's not really a problem. After all, it doesn't hurt to do something even better and be even more confident about it.

For a question that does bother you, you'll see that I've identified three levels of help. They correspond to the three levels that participants in retirement savings plans tend to identify with. Some want the problem solved for them, with no effort on their part ("Do it for me"). Some want education so that they have the necessary principles, as well as guidance in identifying useful questions; then they'll make the required decisions themselves ("Do it with me"). And some want just a little bit of guidance in the background before they solve the problem in their own way ("Help me do it myself").

If you answered "Do it for me" to either of the first two

questions, quite simply, I can't. There isn't a right way to answer them, so I can't say: "Do X and you'll be happy." This is you, this is your life, and only you can decide what will be a good solution for you and make you happy. I don't know you well enough to advise you on how to live Life Two, any more than I can on how to live Life One.

What I can do is what I said in the Preface. I will educate you so that the relevant issues can be clarified, and put you in the driver's seat for deciding on direction and speed.

The third question can actually be answered definitively for some people, those who have enough money that they can budget for their desired lifestyle and buy a guaranteed contract that will provide that level of income for as long as they live. There's a calculator I'll introduce in Walk 18 that will give you an estimate as to whether or not you're one of them.

If you're not, I'll show you how to estimate the income that should be sustainable over your lifetime.

If you're the "Do it with me" type on any of the questions, yes, you've come to the right place. We'll be a team. I'll do the teaching; I'll set you some exercises to show how the learnings apply; and you'll apply them to your own situation. You'll have developed your own customized plan, by the end of the Walking Tour.

And how about "Help me do it myself"? Pretty much the same as "Do it with me," but I expect you'll be much more confident about the relevant issue, and will use the Walks as your way of making sure you haven't missed anything important.

That's it.

DESTINATION

Now you're clear about how to use the different Walks, knowing that their importance to you may vary from Walk to Walk.

EXERCISE

You've already done the exercise, as you've probably guessed. I just wanted to make sure you actually selected a response for each of the three issues.

Complementary stages on the Hoho Bus Tour

Consider taking Stage P7 in the Prologue, about teachable moments and wake-up calls. And perhaps Stage P8 in the Prologue, if you're among the many who aren't completely at home with notions like "per cent" and decimals.

Walk 3

You Need To Become
An Informed Consumer
Of Expertise

WHERE THE ROUTE TAKES US

*You don't need any knowledge before we start. You don't have to be an expert to enjoy Life Two. Sure, some expertise is needed, but you can get that from others. You'll be a consumer of expertise – an **informed** consumer. That makes a big difference.*

THE LEARNING

One more overview piece, this time about the level of knowledge required of you. In a word, none, other than from the education you received before entering Life One.

My goal is to make you an informed consumer of expertise.

This is really important, so I'm going to explain it fully. I hope it'll make you realize that everything you need is within your control. You may just want to skim through it, initially. When you're dealing with, or about to deal with, an expert, that's when the details become more relevant to you.

Again, explicitly: my goal is not to make you an expert, on investment or happiness or anything else. That would take far too long, and isn't necessary. There are experts everywhere. You can be a consumer of their expertise. But I want you to be an informed consumer, so you can use their expertise to best effect. If you want advice, go to an expert and explain your situation and your goals. What I'll give you is education, so you can communicate better with experts and assess the advice they give you.

***

OK, now let me explain what I mean about being an informed consumer of expertise, and why you don't need to be an expert.

In your life, you deal with doctors, you deal with lawyers, you deal with all sorts of experts. And yet you're probably not an expert in any of those fields, and you still cope. The reason is that you don't have to be a doctor to interact with doctors, you don't have to be a lawyer to interact with lawyers, in a useful way.

What you do need is enough information to work with them, to know how to help them to help you. They provide the expertise. You're a consumer, a consumer of their expertise. And you ought to be an informed consumer of their expertise.

To get you to that point, I hope to show you two kinds of things.

Here's the first. It's to give you a framework to put things in. I'll remind you of an analogy I've used before. You know how you see pieces of a jigsaw puzzle, and you wonder how they fit together? It helps a lot if you have the cover of the box that the puzzle comes in, with a picture to show you what the whole thing looks like when it's complete. If you have that picture, it becomes easier to see where any one piece of the puzzle fits. I want to give you that sort of big picture about Life Two. So: the principles that underlie the subject, how they fit together, that sort of thing.

Here's the second thing. What does it mean, exactly, to be an informed consumer of expertise? What does it help you to do, when an expert tells you something, or gives you advice or makes a recommendation for you to follow?

It helps you to do three things. It helps you to assess the expertise, it helps you to challenge the recommendation, and it helps you to apply the principles to your own situation. Again, let me explain what each of those phrases means.

***

(1) Assess the expertise. How do you assess what an expert tells you? To assess means to judge, to evaluate. Well, to do that, you need to understand what are the main messages that the expert is giving you. So, if you don't understand the main conclusions of the expert, say so, and make sure they get explained to you in a way you do understand. For example, every stage in the Walking Tour (and in the Hoho Bus Tour, for that matter) has an explicit destination, a point that you need to understand. Anything an expert tells you should also have a point, one that you understand.

(2) How do you challenge an expert? Well, this is where being informed is important. You need to understand the principles that are behind the recommendation. (And that's the point I hope to get you to.) So, when you see recommendations, make sure you understand the principles on which they're based. Make sure you get the expert to identify those principles.

Also make sure you're told about any research that underlies the recommendations. Where does the research come from? Where's the evidence? Is it based on stuff that's happened in the past? And if so, is the same sort of thing likely to happen in the future?

This is one of the important principles you'll come across in investing. The future may not look like the past. The reason is that investing isn't like the physical world. If you throw a stone upward, it'll rise, then at some point it'll start to fall. That will always happen. It's because of gravity. Gravity pulls physical objects back to the earth. It did it yesterday, it does it today, it'll still do it tomorrow.

Investing isn't like that. Investing involves putting a price on assets and buying and selling, and those prices are based on people interacting with one another. You know how it is with people. There's no guarantee that they'll always act the same way. They're allowed to change their minds, in a way that gravity can't. And so, particularly as new information becomes available, prices change all the time. Investors are trying to anticipate what tomorrow's price is going to be. No one ever gets it right all the time. Getting most of it right in the past, isn't a guarantee of getting most of it right in the future.

For now, it's enough to note that one way in which you can challenge an expert, is to ask what assumptions about the future the expert is making, what other ways are there in which the future can evolve (in other words, what could go wrong), how would the recommendations work out if the future doesn't evolve in the way the expert has assumed? You need to be able to make that sort of challenge, in order to evaluate, to assess, whether you're comfortable with the advice you're getting.

I'm not saying you always have to challenge the expert. I'm just showing you how, if you feel the inclination.

(3) And finally, I said that you ought to be able to see how the advice actually applies to your own situation. In fact, that's the area in which you're the expert. You know your own situation better than the expert does. To make the expert's advice as good as it can be, you need to be able to convey the elements that define your situation to the expert. That way, the expertise can be tailored to fit you, rather than just being off the peg. Not that off the peg is necessarily bad – I don't mean that at all. But the more the expert knows about you, the better the fit.

The expert on any other subject is, in fact, an informed consumer of your own expertise about yourself. So, explain yourself, and the expert will know how to make the advice fit you as well as possible.

**

How do you explain yourself? Let me suggest two things you can do.

(A) One is to paint a picture of success. Imagine yourself (your partner, your family, whoever) several years down the road. What would make you feel that the outcome has been good? There are several categories to think about, as you paint that picture of success. They're actually the focal point of much of the education in this book. But if you can convey to the expert what that picture looks like, that'll help enormously.

As human beings, we're notorious for hoping for way more than is reasonable. Typically, our financial ambitions far exceed our willingness to pay for them, or the amount of risk we're willing to take. That alone is worth discussing with the expert: to see how feasible your definition of success is.

(B) And so, of course, the other thing you can do is to paint a picture of failure. What sort of outcome, several years down the road, would make you feel disappointed? If you can let the expert get inside your head, it might be possible to detect early signs, in the future, that events are working out well or disappointingly. It might be possible to design a Plan B that isn't too difficult or expensive to move to. All kinds of possibilities.

All of this should make you realize how much better you know yourself than the expert knows you. I hope this realization will give you the courage to challenge the expert's advice – something you might otherwise be afraid to do, because after all, they're the expert, right, and what do you know? You know yourself, that's the answer. And so, raise the issue with any expert whose advice doesn't make you comfortable.

**

Anyway, those are the goals. To show you the big picture; and to help you, not to become an expert, but to assess, challenge and apply the expertise that's presented to you. I hope you feel that those are worthwhile objectives, and worth spending time on.

And once more let me remind you that this is not an instruction manual. My purpose is not to tell you: here's what you should do. I don't know you and your circumstances well enough to do that, and your own decisions will be much more compelling and appropriate than anything I can tell you. I'm giving you an education, a frame of reference, one that explains and shows relationships, yet leaves ample scope for thoughtful, informed personal judgment because different people will have different goals and different attitudes. It's not directive. It's "Here's how to think about it," not "There's only one thing you should do."

DESTINATION

You can get all the benefit of the expertise that you need if you're an informed consumer. That means you understand what the expert is telling you, you've asked the expert what principles and assumptions his or her advice is based on, and you've explained to the expert what sort of outcome you'd consider successful and what sort of outcome you'd consider failure.

EXERCISE

Take a first shot at painting those pictures of success and failure. Engage your partner, so that you have something you can both agree on.

Paint, in all, six verbal pictures, looking (let's say) ten years down the road – though of course there's no magic in the number ten, and any period that fits your circumstances better can be used.

What would success look like, in connection with your future life?

What would disappoint you, if your future life turned out that way?

What would a set of day-to-day, or month-to-month, activities look like, for you to feel that you're passing time pleasantly? I don't mean listing the activities, I mean what sort of feelings a pleasant set of activities would give you.

What sort of feelings, in connection with day-to-day or month-to-month activities, would give you the impression that life is boring?

What would financial success like look, for you?

What sort of outcomes would lead you to think that you've failed, financially?

Take your time doing this. It's not a one-hour or overnight exercise. Think about it for days, if you like. That's fine. Doing it is what's important; it's not a test of speed or a contest. And a few sentences are enough – you're not compelled to write a series of essays. The mere fact that you think about these questions is a huge step forward.

Is there anyone you could show these verbal pictures to, whose judgment you trust, without too much embarrassment? That's a tough one. It's OK if there isn't anyone like that. The fact is, just completing this exercise is a huge achievement. You can guess that very, very few people do this – that's how far ahead of the pack you already are.

By the way, like most of the exercises, this is one you might want to repeat periodically – every year, every five years, at special times in your life – whenever.

And don't worry about "getting it right." The fact that you've done this at all will be helpful with future exercises.

Walk 4

Life's Abundance
Is Not Just
About Money

WHERE THE ROUTE TAKES US

Of course we focus a lot on money, because it's easily interchanged into sources of happiness. But we know intuitively that it isn't everything. In addition to a financial portfolio, we have a "life's abundance portfolio." Let's recognize it.

The learning

Let's start with an interview, to show you how one couple is thinking about Life Two.

***

Tour Guide [TG]: Toni and Toby, please introduce yourselves and tell us about your lifestyle.

Toni: I'm Toni, and we retired a few years ago. Or Toby retired a few years ago. I'm a teacher and I retired before him. Then we moved to M [something between a small town and a farming community]. And that's it, really!

Toby: Our grandchildren.

TG: I was about to ask ...

Toby: Yes, our grandchildren are why we moved to M. There's not much to say about our lifestyle, really. We're not role models for anyone.

TG: Tell us what you do all day.

Toni: Nothing much. My brother-in-law jokes that we wake up with nothing to do, and by the end of the day half of it is still undone!

TG: Tell us about your volunteering.

Toby: Well, we spend a lot of time volunteering. We drive old people around, we read to them, we help organize events. The list is never-ending, if you really want to find something to do. And then on top of that we just enjoy being in the country. There are rolling hills all around, and lakes and ponds. We walk the dog, we visit baseball diamonds in the summer and the skating rink in the winter. There's a beautiful cemetery we walk around. And then we got bikes to explore it better. So we actually get a lot of exercise as well.

Toni: And then of course our grandchildren! We always loved visiting them, and after Toby retired we could be even closer. And their parents are happy having us here, because we get along and it lets both of them work. So between the babysitting and taking them to school and bringing them back home – yes, we're really busy!

TG: I'm curious, does your being so involved with raising your grandchildren create conflict with their parents?

Toby: No, because the parents' standards have to apply. We're clear about that. We have the privilege of helping to raise our grandchildren, but that doesn't give us the right to replace their values with ours. Not that there's a real difference.

Toni: You have to have a single set of values. If you don't, kids get confused. And after that they'll exploit the differences – you learn that, as a teacher!

TG: Anything else?

Toni: Actually, a lot more! Our social life extends to the church and a book club and other local social groups. We read a lot. We enjoy our old music. We even go to dances! All in all, it's really busy. But as I said, there's nothing different there that makes us role models for anyone. It works for us.

Toby: It'd be boring for many people. My younger brother, for example. He retired long before us. He made money in his business, that's how he could do it.

TG: Do you mix with his family much?

Toni: We spend Christmas with them. They don't want to travel to "the sticks," and we get a chance to see the Christmas lights in the city and do some shopping. At first they used to make fun of "the country bumpkins," but now they just accept us. They live a much more extravagant life, but I'm not sure they're happier. They seem to always be restless and planning some big adventure in some new foreign place. I guess they don't seem to be content. Their lifestyle seems to us like doing stuff for the sake of doing something. To each his own. It's all in your head, I guess.

Toby: It's my brother's third marriage and my sister-in-law's second. But this one seems to have taken, which is great. And it's mellowed him a bit, I think.

Toni: He's always been someone who is very decisive and always in the right. Now he's willing to admit others can have a valid point of view, even if it's different!

The really nice thing is how the grandchildren get along, when they get together. Our sister-in-law's oldest is a real leader. She's a little older than the others, and she's always got something interesting for them to do. They worship her. What a teacher she'd make, one day!

TG: When you moved to M, did your new life take shape right away?

Toni: No, it took a little while, actually. It's a close community. We felt a bit like outsiders at first, but the church and the book club helped. And of course through our grandchildren and their school activities. We and the other parents and grandparents really connected through them.

TG: Thank you for your story. I don't want to suggest (as you fear) that you're role models. But that's because I wouldn't do that to anybody. We're all different. I just wanted to bring to life the fact that money isn't everything. In fact you didn't even mention money once. We'll leave that for another time. But meanwhile you are the embodiment of the saying that "success is getting what you want, and happiness is wanting what you get."

Toby: That reminds me of something our son said. He's an actuary, and he says it's always important to actuaries, in analyzing experience, to compare the actual experience with what they expected. It's the same with happiness. How happy you are depends not only on what you experience, but on how high you set your expectations.

***

As a geek, there was a time when all I thought about was numbers. And in particular, numbers connected with investment and with pensions, because that was my job, and I loved it. But life is about more than numbers, and about more than money.

Certainly my happiness research brought that home to me.

What I discovered is that money does have a positive influence on happiness. Of course, that's hardly a surprise. But it's not as simple as: more money means more happiness, and lots more money means lots more happiness. It's much more subtle than that.

If there's very little money, and it's all focused just on surviving and making ends meet, then yes, more money means more happiness. But once there's enough money to survive, and the focus changes from surviving to thriving, then typically it takes a lot more money to increase happiness noticeably. And when you have a huge amount of money, having even more money matters very little.

***

Why is this? It's because, once survival is assured, we tend to look around at people we admire (or even envy), and see what they have. And our target is no longer something absolute (like survival), but something relative, something that we compare with what others have. That's why, no matter how much we may have, a relative comparison with others may not enhance our happiness.

But there's something else that hit me between the eyes, because it's so well expressed and I encountered it accidentally.

I was speaking at a conference, and came across another session that looked interesting. It was about financial professionals having successful meetings with clients. And a man named Dr Ed Jacobson laid out a notion that he called the "life's abundance portfolio."[1]

I hope he expands it into a book. It's a reminder that life is about so much more than money. He reminds us that we have all kinds of interactions and experiences in life. I can't remember the labels he used, but here are the words I use to remember his concept. He said there are seven aspects of life to consider. I remember them in pairs:

- family and friends;
- work and play;
- physical health and mental (including spiritual) health;
- and, oh yes, finances.

I think of them as the seven asset classes in your life's abundance portfolio. And when we're considering life's abundance in the way Dr Jacobson suggests, it's clear that money is only one aspect.

Oh wait, that's investment jargon. Let me explain it to you.

A portfolio is a collection of things. So a "life's abundance portfolio" is a collection of things relating to life's abundance. An asset class is a group of things with similar characteristics. So the whole phrase describes all the stuff relating to life's abundance, classifying them under seven headings. In other words, think of everything that makes your life feel full and complete, under the seven headings listed.

I commend Ed's notion to you. I've even suggested to financial professionals (expanding a thought that Ed mentioned) that they use it, right from the start, to establish with their clients that the professional part of what they do is only one aspect of your fulfilled life. So, before they review your financial portfolio, they should review with you your life's abundance portfolio. I add (as Ed did) a practical angle: they need to establish this broader context when the financial side is going well. Otherwise there's a big (and legitimate) danger that you'll view it as a cynical distraction, a way to conceal bad financial news.

All of this allows us to remember how lucky we are in the rest of our life's abundance portfolio. Thank you, Dr Ed Jacobson.

DESTINATION

There's more to life and happiness than money. There's a "life's abundance portfolio."

EXERCISE

Write down the seven components of your life's abundance portfolio. Make some notes about each one.

What do you have in that component?

What's missing?

How would you rate your satisfaction with that component? Just use a simple rating system, like a 1-10 scale or something like that.

What can you do to raise the score in each of them?

That'll help you create a sense of purpose.

Take your time, it's not obvious to any of us as to how to

compile this list. Just by doing this exercise, you will be thinking about your life in much more depth than most people ever get to.

Also, this is something you can come back to. In fact, you should revisit it periodically. It's nice if each revisit causes you to appreciate life more.

COMPLEMENTARY STAGES ON THE HOHO BUS TOUR

Stage F 04 in Route 4 (exploring retirement finance) is a reminder that investing is only a means to an end.

Walk 5

How Best To
Spend Time
And Money

Here's what experts say about how to spend time and money to enhance happiness, recognizing that we actually have two things we can spend: not just money, but also time. Here's how to make the most of both of them, rather than waste them.

THE LEARNING

As we found on Walk 4, it's possible to live a very happy life even if we're not financially wealthy. And research on the intersection of finance and psychology suggests that what creates happiness is experiences, shared experiences, rather than material possessions. That's because, in addition to spending money, we can spend time; and how we spend our time is enormously important.

Now, advice on happiness has become an industry on its own. I'll let you find your own self-help ideas. In serious journals, I found some of the advice in two papers helpful, and not always obvious. Every piece of advice is based on formal sociological experiments, but I'll skip describing the experiments and feed you just the conclusions.

Let me repeat. There's more to spending than money. Because, in fact, all of us have two kinds of resources to spend: money and time. We forget about time as a resource. Economists have focused on money, the retirement industry focuses on money, but income and wealth don't measure everything that we value, as we've just seen.

***

So, how we spend time is important. One paper[2] offered some principles for spending time happily. Here's my selection and my interpretation of four of their principles.

Spend time with the right people. That means family and friends. Loneliness is bad. And here's an interesting angle. Since we spend so much time at work, seeking out friendships at work can be very rewarding.

Spend time on the right things. That means experiences that are likely to be memorable. That doesn't need any further explanation.

Enjoy the experience without spending the time. Daydream! I'll bet you never thought of that – I certainly didn't. But it turns out that just thinking about something pleasurable, activates pleasure-giving chemicals in the brain.

Expand your time. Focus on the present. Be in the zone, doing something challenging, something fulfilling. It makes time seem longer. So does even a few minutes of deep breathing, actually. (All of this is emphasized these days when "mindfulness" is discussed.)

We can all do these things. And even these little hints start to explain why money isn't everything, and why the poor can be as happy as the wealthy.

***

How about the way we spend money? If you think about it, a wealthy person who knows nothing about wine may not assemble any better a wine cellar than someone who has less money. Similarly, if we know nothing about happiness, the way we spend our money may be wasteful, in happiness terms. And it turns out that we're not at all good at anticipating what will make us happy. One academic wrote a whole book about this: *Stumbling on Happiness* by Dan Gilbert.[3]

So here are four more selected lessons, about spending money.[4]

Buy more experiences and fewer things. It turns out that when we look back, it's experiences we remember with pleasure, more than material possessions. What are the things we want to recover first, in a fire or a flood? Typically, photograph albums – our lives, our memories – not material possessions. Of course, today we'd add videos too. And storing everything online is one way to try to make sure we never lose them.

Help others instead of just yourself. Human beings are social animals. People who engage in social spending seem happier than those who don't. And that's not just giving to charity. It also includes giving gifts to friends. As the saying goes: gifts make friends, and friends make gifts.

Buy many small pleasures rather than a few big ones. This is not intuitive. But it's the case that frequent doses of lovely things may make us happier than infrequent doses of lovelier things. Generate those pleasure-giving neurochemicals frequently. Break down a big experience into a series of smaller ones.

Follow the herd instead of your head, sometimes. Since we're not good at anticipating what makes us happy, we might do better to go with what others, who have actually made selections from those choices, feel after the event.

DESTINATION

Experts give us some unexpected insights into how to spend time and money to enhance our happiness.

EXERCISE

Revisit the exercise that you did after Walk 4. Does Walk 5 suggest anything else to you, to add to your sense of purpose? As you'll recognize by now, there are no right or wrong answers, just answers that appeal to you.

Walk 6

Is Retirement
Complicated—
Or Is It Scary?

WHERE THE ROUTE TAKES US

You'll see that you're not alone in thinking that transitioning to Life Two is scary. Once you understand that, the fear typically goes away. You just need to take the first step. Let me show you how to confront and overcome your fear.

The learning

In my mind I imagine the typical reader thinking: "It's so complicated! I wouldn't even know where to start." A friend wrote to me saying he expects that more people would describe it as "so scary." He added: "I wonder if 'it's so complicated' is really cover for 'I'm scared' and if framing it as the latter helps connect with readers at a more intimate level early on."

I think he's right. And so he got me thinking. How would I address a reader who's scared? Maybe something along these lines ...

***

It's a natural feeling to be scared. It's not anything to be ashamed of.

Dr Daniel Crosby, a clinical psychologist who is far better qualified than me to opine on this, says that retirement can bring out our worst feelings:[5] thinking about death, having to rely on investment returns rather than the regular pay slip, and yes, ignorance on a most important subject. What people crave, he adds, are characteristics like simplicity, safety, certainty. They're all gone, after retirement. Scared? Who wouldn't be?

It's also natural to feel sad. Dr Harry Levinson, psychologist, reminds us: "All change is loss, and all loss must be mourned."[6] The change from work to retirement is a profound change (which is why many would rather do it in steps rather than a one-shot jump off a cliff), and mourning the loss of the previous lifestyle for its familiarity and stimulus and companionship is not just normal but recommended and helpful.

So take your time and realize there's bound to be a transition, and there ought to be a transition.

As you think about the next stage in your life, let me explicitly address some of your fears. Forgive me: in writing this I don't mean to put words into your mouth, but I need to capture some of those fears.

***

I'm afraid of the unknown.

Yes, the future is unknown. It's unknowable, almost by definition. What do we know about retirement? Often, very little. Well, we know how it ends: in death. And that can trigger negative thoughts. Remember when we were young? If something scared us, we imagined monsters, which then made it all even more scary, because now the unknown felt powerful and sinister. Of course, it never turned out to be that bad! Thinking about retirement can be like that: "I'll have nothing to do, I'll be a nobody, I'll fade away." No, it won't be like that. So let me encourage you to be young again, in another way.

When we're young and think about the future, we fill it with our dreams. Well, we're never too old to dream. This stage should be (as Dr Laura Carstensen of Stanford University calls it) the "autumn crescendo" of our lives,[7] the time when dreams are fulfilled. And the time available for fulfillment may be much longer than you think. (Later on, in Walk 13, I'll give you an idea of how long.) I encourage you to dream again.

We already know that our brains are hard-wired for us to feel happiest in our later years, whether we're working or retired or something in between. Don't fight it! Thinking about more than just money, spending time and money constructively (Walks 4 and 5): those ideas all expand your perspective and make you realize that it's not an unknown world; rather, it's one you're aware of but never thought about explicitly.

***

I'm afraid of change.

Yes, there'll be a change. That's inevitable. That's why not thinking about it is the worst way to deal with it, because then things happen to you, rather than happening because you want them to.

Think about what you'd like to do, what you'd enjoy doing. I'll have a specific Walk dedicated to helping you with this.

You'll also learn that it won't be a sudden, overnight change, it'll be a gradual transition. Complementary stages on the Hoho Bus Tour, listed at the end of this Walk, tell you more about that.

Even better, you can do something about it. There are books, there are websites on the internet and other tools that help. I'll show you some of that wisdom on this Walking Tour.

If you are inclined to deep, existential thoughts, I'll take you on a Walk that helps you to think about who you really are. One reader wrote to me: "I think you've been reading my mind ... I'm scared not of the financial element, more of loss of identity." Another expanded on this: "We have, over our working careers, had something – a title, an occupation or a profession – that has provided us with an identity. But retirement threatens to take all of that away, and we are left wondering what will be left when that is gone. That can be very scary."

If you're wondering what you might actually do in retirement, yet another Walk helps take you from random stray thoughts to planning a new life.

But it'll never happen the way you plan, right? Yes, right, as far as some aspects are concerned. That doesn't actually matter. Making the plan is what's important, because then, when things don't turn out exactly the way you hoped, you'll have done enough thinking to be able to adapt the plan. Military people know that no battle plan ever survives its first contact with the enemy. Don't expect your dreams to be totally fulfilled. That's normal, not a failure.

Don't think of things as "right" or "wrong." "Right" suggests there's only one possible answer, and everything else is "wrong." Instead, think of things as "good" or "better" rather than "right." That change in mindset helps generate joy when things go better, rather than regret that they're not perfect.

I think of giving up full-time work as mentally moving to a new land. Like going to school for the first time, or to university, or entering a new relationship, or starting a job. You've done it before. It's scary. It's also an opportunity to reinvent yourself. And in this new land, you already know the language and the culture, family and friends are still there (even if you lose contact with some workmates) – even pets are still there. It's not like a physical move.

And, as Dr Levinson said, it's OK to grieve. For most, it takes time to transition to a new life. I'm not making this up: it happened to me. Even though I tried as much as I could to make it at least a partial continuation of my old lifestyle, it turned out that when I finally had the courage to move – physically to a different city – it took three years before I felt that the new one was really home, and I stopped yearning for the old place. I had to build a whole new social life. Only when that expanded to fill my time, and felt comfortable, was I able to revisit the old place happily and enjoy it, and then happily return "home."

***

I'm scared that I know nothing about this big, complicated subject. And I'm scared to show how ignorant I am.

Yes, those are natural feelings. I hope I can persuade you that they're unnecessary. First, if you're scared of your ignorance, you're in the vast majority, so revealing it says nothing negative about you. Join the crowd! Second, remember what I said in Walk 2 about expertise: I hope it'll make you realize that in your mind you're setting the bar too high. You don't need to be an expert. You only need to know enough to become an informed consumer of expertise. And that's what you'll be, after this tour. That's my goal for you.

Not that you might not seek help anyway. If you want to do so, there are a number of Walks and stages that assist you to get that help, which could be psychological or financial.

***

You've forgotten about the fear of losing the certainty of the regular paycheck and relying on investment returns, which are uncertain and something else I know nothing about.

Oh, sorry about that. That's actually an easy one. In fact there are two different ways to deal with it. Both involve generating an income stream from your assets. In one case the stream is as regular and as guaranteed as a paycheck. In the other case (and you can choose which case you want) it can be made just as regular, but the amount is less certain, in the hope that it'll eventually turn out to be bigger. Your choice. I'll show you how all that stuff works on Walk 21, with lots more detail available, if you want it, on the Hoho Bus Tour.

***

Ideally, this is the best phase of life, and you find peace within yourself.

But first you have to be willing to get there.

Most people find – eventually – that the best way to deal with fear is to face it. Once you face the fear, it stops growing. Typically you find it's manageable. And then it's a relief to stop running away from it. And new vistas open up as you proceed.

There's an old saying: a journey of a thousand miles begins with a single step.

I hope I've encouraged you to take that first step, by showing you the kinds of things you'll encounter on this Walking Tour and the problems you'll solve along the way. Read on!

DESTINATION

Being scared is natural. Once you understand why, and what you can do about it, the fear typically goes away. As I've said before: just take the first step.

EXERCISE

This Walk has a number of complementary stages on the Hoho Bus Tour, listed below. Pick the ones that interest you and read them, so that you can relate to the issues more deeply.

COMPLEMENTARY STAGES ON THE HOHO BUS TOUR

I mentioned that moving to Life Two is typically not a sudden, overnight change; rather, it's a gradual transition. You can learn about the ways in which others have transitioned to retirement, their patterns of behavior in retirement, their spending patterns. On the website I describe my own unanticipated experience of transition in Stage H 22 in Route 1 (exploring happiness and the psychology of Life Two). It's not just me. Experts have observed – learn lessons from them. Stage H 31 in Route 1 identifies six lessons for a successful retirement, and Stage H 32 in Route 1 describes four types of retiree behavior patterns. Stage H 44 in Route 1 tells of a couple who performed a retirement dry run.

Walk 7

Reinventing
Yourself In A
New Land

WHERE THE ROUTE TAKES US

Entering Life Two is scary, particularly because we don't think about it until it gets near, and then there's little time to adjust. But it's also an opportunity to reinvent yourself. Learn from the dreams and hopes and fears of others – and from your own experience, because you may actually have done something similar before.

THE LEARNING

Many panelists in our pre-Walk interview, this time. I asked them to think about life after full-time work now, while they're still working. In some cases this was the first time they had given it any thought (though I think they were pretty coherent). I've artificially assembled portions from several separate interviews into a mock panel interview, changing and combining some details so that the interviewees don't get recognized. Think of this as fiction based on fact.

***

Tour Guide: I've chatted with many of you about your plans once full-time work stops for you. And so I've asked some of you to join me up here and tell everyone what you told me.

Panelist 1: I'm not yet 40, so that's a long way into the future, for me. But I admit I'm already worried about retirement. I'd like to retire young. It's the freedom – not having to be somewhere every day, not even having to answer to anyone – go to the gym, run errands, whatever. There are happinesses associated with working, but for me working is just a means to an end. I'm not sure I want to work for the sake of working. Ask me in 20 years and maybe I'll have an answer!

But I worry about what I'll do with my time, after work. Not every career gives you the opportunity to keep doing the same thing part-time. So I'll have to be proactive and take responsibility for my life. And I'll have to link my life's psychology to my physical health, whatever it is at the time. That's as far as I've got.

Panelist 2: Well, my husband and I are a little bit older than 40! We're hoping to retire in the near future. And on our vacation this year we discussed the sort of things we'd like to do. It's good to find out that we're in agreement!

Much as we love each other, we need social interaction. We can only be with each other a certain amount of time before we need to be with other people!

We hope we'll have a good relationship with our kids and the partners they choose, but that's not within our control. Like my husband's parents. They let us live with them in the early years and save money, but they never interfered with our life plans. Whereas my mother kept telling me what to do – probably because that's what she got from her mother.

What will we actually do? We want to avoid cold winters – maybe vacation together with another family (like my brother's family). Volunteering. My husband coaches sports. Me with the church. A hospice too, now that I've seen a friend who needed one. Some fundraising for good causes.

And be grandparents! Please! Spoil our grandchildren! Seriously, help our children if they need us to help with raising grandchildren.

Do fun drives and camping. See the country and the countryside. We've always loved doing that.

Panelist 3: Retirement, like university, is about graduating to a new future. (I remember you used that expression in a presentation!) I want to help people who aren't wealthy. I want to get into public speaking, it's so very powerful, to share with others what you've learnt. Just as I like listening, to learn from the experiences of my colleagues, who may think of me as a daughter or a sister when they talk. Even now, my friends have younger siblings about to go to university – they listen to me more because I'm closer to their age and I've had the experience more recently. What's useful is "If I could go back, here's what I'd do differently" – and that's mostly to keep a balance, don't get all caught up in one thing.

I have a younger brother (there's a big age gap) just going into high school. We had our first serious conversation. He's interested in investing, and had no idea there's someone in the family who works in the business. I want to bring him into the office, etc. Even if he doesn't end up in the business, he'll learn so much from being around it.

It makes me happy to have some impact in kids' lives. Sometimes they need an outside third party, because they're not inclined to listen to their parents. It helps the kids to find themselves, just to have someone to talk to.

It isn't just kids. One of my clients has friends but none that he's willing to talk to about his life, so he talks to me. It helps just to tell him there are lots of people in that position. Chatting about his daughters – I can't give him advice, just how to think about the situation. It's not just about investment questions.

Sorry, I've gone off track, talking about life in general rather than about retirement. Thinking about retirement excites me. I want to gather other people's experiences so I can enjoy my own experiences – a huge field where I have the freedom to go wherever I want.

Panelist 4: I want two things when I retire. First, enough money to enjoy myself in the first few years. Then, when I'm decrepit, I won't need as much, but I want enough to survive.

About our planned transition. My wife wants a retirement job of some kind, with no pressure to take home at night, to get paid "mad money" with some flexibility in working hours. Me, I want to apply my knowledge by "giving back" – I don't care about being paid, I just want my expenses covered. I think I'm appreciated as a knowledge worker. And my employer has been good to me, so I'd like to make myself available to them rather than go somewhere else.

I'd like to write! I need to develop the discipline to do that. I think of stories – fiction – I think of an unexpected outcome and work my way to that. It's not to become a famous author, it's just for the pleasure of writing. Maybe I'll take a creative writing course.

Where will we live? Our house is too big. Live near our grandchildren? There's no guarantee our son will stay where he is. So we're tentatively planning to go back to the town where we came from – our family origins – but we'll have to re-establish close relations with them.

When? 55. Why 55? Scared of either physical or cognitive decline. I've seen it with aunts and uncles – late 60s, early 70s, and then they couldn't enjoy life any more. You don't live to work, you work to live.

Panelist 5: I told my husband: if we get to $X, I'll stop working. He said: no you won't, you like it too much! But even though I don't show it at work, things do get to me sometimes. The thing is, whatever I do, my heart has to be in it.

I'm not sure I could stop cold turkey. Maybe in the next five years we'll be able to afford it, but I don't like big change. I've been lucky, even with a couple of work changes – it's never been difficult, finding something good. I could even go back to being a bank teller, the way I used to be.

TG: Let's stop there, for now. What a fascinating exposure to philosophies of life! And it's those philosophies that will either be put to the test or enable us to cope, as we graduate from full-time work.

***

I've said many times that Life Two is like moving to a new land, the land of personal freedom. You'll probably be afraid of the move, as with any other major move in your life.

Like it or not, it's a land that requires total immersion. You're not a tourist. You're not an ex-pat, who wants to live in the new land and expand your experiences and your mind, but with the comforting knowledge that you'll go back. (Though, like many ex-pats, you may find you'd rather stay on. Perhaps that's a good starting attitude!)

So, in this Walk, let's examine what's involved in the move, and what opportunities it offers for reinventing yourself, collecting ideas from the earlier Walks.

***

The best part of the move is what it doesn't entail.

You already know the language. You already know the culture; no culture shock for you.

Your family and close friends are still with you. (Your

workmates may not be. Some retirees find that their exclusion from work-related daily events means that they and their former workmates no longer have anything in common.) And your pets are still with you.

You don't need to make new housing or banking arrangements, or sign up for utilities or internet connections. You don't have to worry afresh about personal safety in a new land.

No logistical challenges, no bureaucracy and legal requirements to learn about, no need to search for where you buy groceries.

No new currency.

You get the idea. This is so much easier than moving physically.

***

And yet it is a move, even if the move is mental rather than physical. And that's why you'll probably be scared and miss many aspects of your previous life, and (in a way) feel homesick.

That's OK. It's more than OK – it's natural. The fact is that all change is loss, and all loss must be mourned. (As a specific case study, you might already have checked out Stage H 22 in Route 1 on the Hoho Bus Tour, in which I share with you some of my own feelings in my transition to this new land, when I was unprepared for them.) It's par for the course – the exception is to slide smoothly into giving up full-time work as if nothing has changed, because typically a lot changes.

Nevertheless, this transition is a teachable moment. It's a time when we're naturally willing to give the change some thought. And as it's a major change, it's also an opportunity – an opportunity to be proactive, in fact an opportunity to reinvent ourselves. That's not necessary, of course – I'm just saying that it's an occasion when this is more than usually possible. And even if we don't want to reinvent ourselves, the way of thinking about the move is pretty much the same as the way to think about reinventing ourselves.

Did you move away from home when you went to university? Did you move in the course of work? On both occasions, you were forced to explore what the new place offered. Did you take the opportunity to change something about yourself? See – you've already done this before.

*****

Here are some things to consider:

Accept that it's a new place. Even though you'll feel homesick, get over hating everything unfamiliar. Get support. Search for helpful websites and publications.

You may want to check out Dr Laura Carstensen's notion of this being a turning point in your life (see the Complementary Stages, at the end of this Walk). This may be the autumn of your life, but you can make it the autumn crescendo rather than a fade-away.

An encore career? But this time it would probably be a deeply personal one, more focused on satisfying yourself than on making money. Satisfying community needs? Mentoring young people?

How about education for the pure pleasure of learning? Linked to travel, perhaps?

Is this the time to focus on your health, the way you never had time to, before?

Remember the non-financial parts in Dr Ed Jacobson's "life's abundance portfolio" in Walk 4: family and friends; work and play; physical health and mental (including spiritual) health. Did you rate your satisfaction under each of those six headings? Did your self-assessments suggest areas where it would be productive (meaning, where it would increase your happiness) if you did something differently?

If one of the possibilities is actually a physical move to a new place, what about a dry run? Try out the new place on vacation before making the commitment. Make the dry run not just financial but also psychological, imagining that you have actually made a permanent move, to get the best chance of seeing if you can adapt happily.

Perhaps you need a mentor, a friend, a companion, to share the journey? And when you do undertake the journey, you could use social media to share your plans and experiences, and learn from the experiences of others.

Remember to focus on shared experiences, and on many small things rather than on one big thing – more happiness comes that way.

If you already have a passion for someone or something, that's likely to be a focal point and a way of feeling a sense of fulfillment. What if you don't? Is there a way to get to fulfillment regardless? Yes there is. It's a sense of purpose, of achievement, that gets you there. And typically the purpose (even if you don't realize it) is to live on in the minds of others, to be remembered happily after you're gone. It's answering the question "Who do you want to be?" rather than "What do you want to do?"

In turn, that suggests two possible paths:

Your family. The closest thing you'll ever have to physical immortality on this earth is your children. If succeeding generations have something to remember you for, and to remember you by, you'll live on in their minds after you've departed. This is one reason why grandchildren are so important to us.

Volunteering or mentoring. When you help others, you not only get enormous satisfaction from it, you also live on in their minds.

And finally, a reminder of some psychological angles to support you when things don't go the way you hoped or anticipated.

Don't be scared when you fail, or when something takes an unexpected turn. Expect the occasional setback. You'll learn from it, not only about the thing itself, but about yourself.

Remember that the details of the proposed plan will inevitably give way to new ideas as you put the details into practice. That's not failure in your plan, that's the triumph of experience over your imperfect imagination.

It takes time to adjust, to get used to the new land, to see which aspects you like. This isn't a rush job – it's building up to the autumn crescendo. Give it time to build.

It's also OK not to have a passion for anything. Again, it's not a failure, it's a success if you find contentment in a lifestyle that doesn't have a dominant, driving force. How often have you heard that life is a journey rather than a destination? Enjoy the journey.

There's more in the next few Walks and on the Hoho Bus Tour, with specific steps you can take. Meanwhile, I hope this helps. And ultimately it's only your verdict that counts, as far as your happiness is concerned, nobody else's.

DESTINATION

When you leave full-time work behind, it's both scary and an opportunity. Our interview shows only that people are different and have different dreams and hopes and fears. But isn't it nice to dream! And remember, you have probably made this type of transition before.

EXERCISE

Think of whether you've done this before – like going to university, or moving for a new job. Think of the angles suggested in the stage: an encore career, community service, mentoring, further education, travel, a focus on your health, family involvement. Do any of these appeal to you? Do they give you ideas for the future? Make notes. This isn't set in concrete, by any means – these are just ideas that occur to you, while you're focused on reinventing yourself.

And let me remind you: in doing these exercises, you're going much further than most people ever do. You may not realize it, but one of the qualities you're showing is that of leadership.

COMPLEMENTARY STAGES ON THE HOHO BUS TOUR

Stage H 03 in Route 1 (exploring happiness and the psychology of Life Two) gives you details about Dr Laura Carstensen's notion of this being a turning point that leads to the autumn crescendo of your life. And Stage H 22 in Route 1 is mentioned again, as it was after Walk 6.

Take A Breath

Before you move on to the next Walk, take a breath. Think about this: you've visited the neighborhood in Life Two in which others who were afraid of the transition have shared their fears, their experiences and their lessons. There were lots of people in that neighborhood! And now you're much more knowledgeable about the reality of transition than you were before. Getting rid of irrational fears caused by lack of familiarity with a subject is a big deal. There may be more to do. But you can move forward with a surer step.

RECOGNIZE YOURSELF...
AND YOUR PARTNER

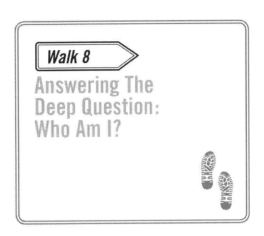

Walk 8

Answering The
Deep Question:
Who Am I?

WHERE THE ROUTE TAKES US

This Walk may or may not be for you. Some (but not all) of us feel defined by our work. Life Two cuts us off from that definition, and it can be disorienting. If that's not you, skip this and move to Walk 9. If it is you, here's help. Defining yourself is a challenge at any time, one that few of us have ever needed to undertake. Here are some questions to ask yourself, the answers to which will give you the necessary insights into who you are.

THE LEARNING

We've seen that this transition is both scary and a chance to reinvent yourself. Of course it's rarely feasible to be able to shed everything about your past and start from scratch. Reinvention is only sincere if it builds on who you really are. Few of us ever consider that explicitly. Defining ourselves is either unnecessary or embarrassing. But this may be a teachable moment in your life. At any rate, you're reading this! And so you're willing to take a shot at answering the question "Who am I?"

There's no instant answer. Not even for those who feel defined by their work or their status in society, which they're proud of and happy with. It's understandable that they wouldn't voluntarily want to give it up. But if that's forced on you – then what? I don't know who you are – you're the one who has to answer the question – but in this Walk I can give you an approach to get started.

And of course it isn't necessary to wait until you're on the verge of retirement. This is an exercise you can undertake any time.

I know whereof I speak. In my case … Well, I can show you how some of the principles involved affected me.

***

George Russell, who felt more like my mentor than my boss, periodically took his senior management team on offsite exercises, to improve us both as managers and as human beings. I remember one in the early 1990s. Stephen Covey had recently published his *7 Habits of Highly Effective People*[8] and I had read it and enjoyed it. George engaged a Covey coach to take us through several exercises based on the book.

At the end of the first day we were given an overnight assignment, to be completed individually. Write your personal mission statement.

That's "Who am I?" but just in a slightly different form, because your mission is your purpose in life, and it's tough to distinguish you from your mission and purpose.

I vividly remember three of the steps we were told might be useful.

The first was easy. Who are the people in history you admire? And why? The answers might cast some light on your aspirations, the person you'd like to be. OK.

The next was a bit closer to home. Among people you know, whom do you admire, and why? A simple question, and for most people probably not the question to trigger an intense, cathartic release of emotion.

But it did, for me. My wife and I were going through a very rough patch in our marriage, threatening its survival. (Our children were well aware of this. I'm saying nothing they don't know. It made life very uncomfortable for them.) We were both extremely unhappy. (Coincidence or not, I was around 50 at the time, close to the traditional age when happiness is lowest.) And the catharsis arose because I realized that my wife is one of the people I most admire, for several qualities she has.

Tears flowed. The floodgates opened. Pent-up emotions that had been building for months, for years, were released.

The tears continued through the next and final step. Imagine your memorial service. A family member, a friend and a co-worker will speak. What would you like them to say, honestly?

Many more tears were shed that night. But I wrote down what I'd like them to say, and from that flowed the behavior I needed to exhibit, and indeed my mission as a human being, a family man, a friend, a member of the community and a co-worker. The pieces came together, building from the bottom up rather than as a great revelation, to help me define who I wanted to be – and clearly was not, at the time.

I don't remember what else there might have been in the prescribed process. Those three steps have imprinted themselves vividly in my mind. (Actually, you might want to check out Covey's book, in case I have mis-remembered the steps he suggested.)

I hope they help you too.

Incidentally, our marriage survived and has thrived, though it took time and therapy. I feel this is our second marriage – we just never formalized a break-up. I showed this Walk to my wife. She said she admired me too, she just didn't like me very much then.

***

Richard Owen, the creator of the website Booming Lives, drew my attention to the Japanese concept of "ikigai," meaning (roughly) a sense of purpose, a reason for being.[9] He says that research shows that the two most vulnerable times in a person's life are the first twelve months after birth and the year following retirement. He adds that people who enter retirement without refreshing their sense of purpose can suffer ill-health, broken relationships and worse. So the first step to a carefree retirement is to think about what the purpose of your retirement will be.

That's where ikigai comes in. Owen says that the Japanese would recommend that you ask yourself these four questions:

1. What do you love?
2. What are you good at?
3. What makes you financially secure?
4. In what way can you make a difference?

Good questions! They helped me to realize that this book and the accompanying website are part of my sense of ikigai, my road towards self-actualization.

***

There are many other ways to prompt "Who am I?" thoughts. I came across another set of three powerful questions[10] when writing *The Retirement Plan Solution*, and my co-authors and I included them there.

You have all the money you need. How would you live your life?

You've just found out you have five to ten years to live. How will you change your life?

You've just found out you have 24 hours to live. What are your regrets?

I think the questions are profound. They force you consider, in succession, what you want to have, what important things you want to do, and who you want to be. That's powerful!

***

There's no measure of success of life as a human being. Ultimately it's not dying rich that establishes a scorecard. Some of us can leave a financial legacy, some can't. We can all leave an emotional legacy, in the way people remember us.

***

Even though success is not a number, I do recall one numerical story about defining oneself. It's a joke, of course. I was a teenager and couldn't stop laughing. It was told by Peter Cook, in the revue Beyond the Fringe, and he was explaining that he never had the Latin that was needed to become a judge, so he became a coal miner instead. Unlike the very rigorous judging exams, "the mining exams aren't very rigorous. In fact, there's a complete absence of rigor. They only ask you one question. They say: 'Who are you?' And I got 75% on that."

DESTINATION

Defining yourself can be an emotional as well as a deep experience. But it's worthwhile.

EXERCISE

Select the approach in Walk 8 that most appeals to you, and follow through. It may be writing your personal mission statement. Or using "ikigai" to ask yourself its four questions. Or answering the three deep questions posed about life and regrets.

In fact, this too is an exercise you may want to revisit periodically, either to revise your responses (life sometimes causes us to change our views, and that's OK) or perhaps to use one of the other approaches for a different perspective.

COMPLEMENTARY STAGES ON THE HOHO BUS TOUR

Stage H 53 in Route 1 (exploring happiness and the psychology of Life Two) considers those who are wedded to their current lifestyle and work identity. Stage H 54 in Route 1 then discusses a relatively new group of helpers: life coaches.

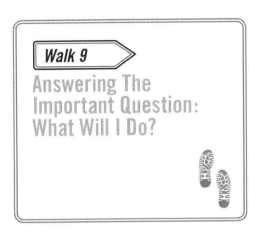

Walk 9

Answering The
Important Question:
What Will I Do?

WHERE THE ROUTE TAKES US

The other important (indeed, almost a perennial) question is: what will I do with my time? You need leisure activities as well as activities related to your mission or purpose. This Walk also reminds you that, if you have a partner, there are two of you involved, not just you.

THE LEARNING

There's no natural dividing line between who you are and what you do. The two aspects fit together. Deciding who you are leads naturally to patterns of behavior consistent with who you are, and designed to achieve the mission, the purpose, that you define for yourself.

But there has to be leisure as well as mission-related activity. You need to renew yourself, reinvigorate yourself, to keep the mission going. There will be others who are comfortable living without a mission. They too must fill their time. This Walk is about that level of activity.

**

A reminder first that there may be two people to consider, if you have a partner. (We'll go into more detail about this on the next Walk.) Though you're a team, you're also two individuals. There are times when you need separate space. Moving to Life Two is an adjustment, a transition, for both of you, not just for you. Your partner isn't used to having you around all day.

I'm reminded of my inlaws, John and Margaret, when John retired. Margaret actually used the cliché: "I married you for better or for worse, but not for lunch." So John created a den for himself above their garage, and when he wasn't out (swimming or playing golf, for example) he stayed there and came "home" for lunch and after the "working" day was over.

I suggested to my wife Susan that her mother was being a bit extreme. Not so, she said. Susan reminded me that I had a private office at work. (This was before the days when the open plan concept took over.) "Suppose I were to come to your office every day. I'd sit and read, or potter around. I wouldn't disturb you. I wouldn't talk to you. Would my presence distract you?"

Ah. I got it. The home was her mother's office, and any other presence in it would be distracting.

Also, as you make plans for yourself, see if and how they

overlap with your partner's. You may not have spent much casual time together over the years, other than on vacation. Here's an opportunity to build constructive togetherness.

***

When I googled "reinvent yourself" I came across the Get-a-Life Tree. Many people used it, and gave credit online for it to Ernie Zelinski and his book *How to Retire Happy, Wild, and Free: retirement wisdom that you won't get from your financial advisor.*[11] There's no substitute for reading it oneself, so I downloaded the latest edition, a bit apprehensive about that word "wild." I needn't have worried.

Zelinski writes about what I call Route 1 on the Hoho Bus Tour, but because he doesn't have to condense it to include Routes 2, 3 and 4, he has a much freer and more expansive treatment of the subject. Actually he covers broadly similar territory to mine, and comes to much the same principles, which is an encouragement and a relief to me. But he does it much better, frankly. I wish I could write like him. He writes clearly and sincerely, with much humor, with tons of stories. The best teachers don't just have substance, they are also entertainers and story-tellers. Place Zelinski among them.

And "wild"? I think he means "carefree, with child-like exuberance." Not "crazy."

I suggest you use his Get-a-Life Tree to help make the transition from a general notion (your new life) to a series of tasks that constitute an action plan.

***

Write things down, because our memories are imperfect. But not in a list. Draw a tree.

A list is linear. It just goes downward. That makes it difficult to connect ideas. Even more, it's difficult for ideas and connections to jump out at you. So draw a tree, says Zelinski, with branches and leaves that spread out in all directions and make overlapping easy.

Use a blank page, and in the middle, in a box, record the goal, theme or objective. You might start, for example, with: options for my retirement.

Draw a big X across the page, with the box at the intersection. Those are four branches of the tree. Along them, write the principal ideas relating to the objective. Whatever the fourth idea, there are usually three useful ones: activities that turn you on now; activities that turned you on in the past; activities that you have thought about doing.

Let me show you an example I found on the internet. You might use something more specific in the box at the intersection.

Fill out what occurs to you regarding each branch, as secondary branches. These could give rise to a third level, and so on.

Zelinski suggests that you generate at least 50 things along the first three branches, no matter how frivolous the ideas may seem – this is a time not for judgment but just for capturing thoughts. Don't stop at 49. Take a couple of days to get there; this is not a rush. Your mind will work overnight, while you sleep, to be creative – in fact, the little-known secret of creativity is to remove the subject from your conscious mind and let your subconscious take over.[12]

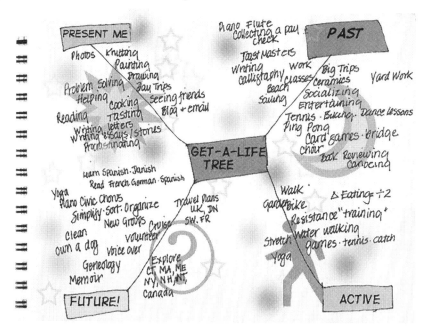

If you have other special categories of activities you want to pursue, perhaps use the fourth branch for that. "Travel," "physical fitness," stuff like that. They may need a page of their own. You get the idea.

If an idea occurs in more than one category, that's great, because it means you've identified a leisure activity that may be a priority in your life. Draw connections. Use colors and images. Zelinski's book gives you far more details than I have copied to this Walk.

One final note.

You're still having trouble getting to 50, even after several days? Guess what, Zelinski can help you there too. He lists over 300 retirement pursuits to add to your list. I love his last one. "Expand this list to 500 activities to outdo me."

I think you can see how his Get-a-Life Tree can help you to identify and prioritize activities for your future day-to-day life.

I'm so glad I got his book. It will be useful to me personally, way beyond this stage.

***

Some thoughts occur to me, to mesh your activities with your mission.

Your mission is at a higher level than your activities, but they should be consistent. Your activities should include things pertaining to the roles you've identified for your mission. They should not just be time-consuming activities to relieve boredom. Nor should they be focused on work-related things like striving for material gain and status. A really good meshing will encompass the full scope your life's abundance portfolio – that's far more likely to make it consistent with "Who am I?"

Enjoy it. Remember: don't judge yourself. Things are not "right" or "wrong." This is enjoyment of a journey, not measuring progress towards a destination.

If you do all this, you'll find that Life Two is truly not the last of life, but the best of it. This will be the real you, coming into flower, perhaps for the first time.

DESTINATION

Now you know how to create a plan, activities that you'll enjoy that are consistent with who you are, and which also take your partner into account.

EXERCISE

Go ahead, use the idea behind the Get-a-Life Tree. This will take you some time, over a period. So it's an ongoing exercise, until you are satisfied that you've come up with stuff that will occupy your time happily. If your own imagination isn't enough to get you there, consider getting the book (which by the way I have no connection with) – it's filled with great ideas.

The reward for completing this exercise is that you'll start to feel that Life Two is like a sabbatical, an extended vacation – but not (horrors!) a permanent vacation.

COMPLEMENTARY STAGES ON THE HOHO BUS TOUR

Stage H 43 in Route 1 (exploring happiness and the psychology of Life Two) goes into more detail on the idea that making a plan is important, even though you know that no plan ever works out perfectly. We mentioned this in Walk 6.

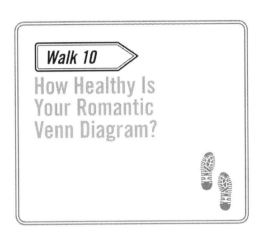

Walk 10

How Healthy Is Your Romantic Venn Diagram?

WHERE THE ROUTE TAKES US

This Walk is important if you have a partner; otherwise skip it and go to Walk 11. Let's expand on the reminder that we're all different, we're all individuals. Even in marriage, we still retain our own personalities. This Walk focuses on times when it's important to recognize those differences.

THE LEARNING

Here's my somewhat unconventional advice to newlyweds.

Make a circle with each hand, using your thumb and forefinger. Move your hands together until the circles overlap partially. (A Venn diagram, most young couples recognize. There's a picture of one here.)

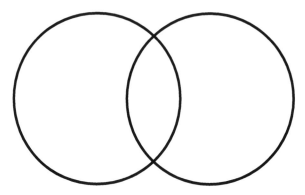

Think of one circle as representing your interests, and the other circle as representing your partner's interests. There's an overlapping area, in addition to the outer parts of the two circles; the overlapping area represents your shared interests.

When you first met, you probably went all soppy over the things you enjoy in common. And more and more of your lives will be spent in that overlapping area of your Venn diagram.

Typically what happens is that you have children, and gradually they take over that area, perhaps even to the extent that the two outside areas no longer have anything in them (except your work). And that's dangerous, because one day the children leave, and sometimes couples find that they no longer have anything in common, and that can lead to instability in the relationship or even divorce.

So, on each anniversary, when you hold each other close and express your love in whatever way suits you, the most romantic words you can tell each other are these: "Honestly, all the parts of our Venn diagram are healthy."

***

Our son tells me that the Venn diagram is still remembered by the friends who attended his wedding. Yes, that's what the father of the groom told the guests. I had promised him that I wouldn't use PowerPoint and wouldn't say anything about him, to which he very properly said, "Anything you say will embarrass me anyway, so go ahead and say whatever you like." He also adds that he and his wife now find the Venn diagram useful to classify their attitude to vegetables!

This isn't wisdom that occurred naturally to me – my mind isn't that wise – but a friend mentioned it when we were chatting at the 40th anniversary of our university matriculation,[13] and I've thought of it gratefully ever since.

***

I mention it here because I think it applies not only in marriage but also in Life Two. And in particular, at three possible times.

The first time is right at the start of Life Two. That's an opportunity to re-shape your life, to reinvent yourself, as many Walks have emphasized. And if you have slowly grown apart, retirement could become a wake-up call to one of the partners. No matter what the specific cause (boredom, money issues, sex, whatever) the empty overlapping part of the Venn diagram draws attention to it. Linda Melone[14] advises what you can do before it's too late: put the relationship first (to me, that means keeping all the parts of your Venn diagram healthy), take care of yourself, assess your role in the problem, talk about sex, talk about everything else too.

The second time potentially comes when two people are thrown together by circumstances later in life, and they discover so strong a mutual appeal that they decide to live the remainder of their lives together. Filling what might have been a void in each life is a wonderful feeling, and the couple's overlapping area is now overflowing with love and joy. But typically each brings an existing family into the new relationship, two non-overlapping parts of their new Venn diagram, and it's not unusual for these two parts not to care for each other, and to cause financial complications. This leads to tensions and conflicts for the couple, who might want to live only in the overlapping area but can't. Advice to second-time-around couples tends to stress taking time, and seeking financial advice, before commitment.[15]

The third time is even later, and it comes if one partner becomes the caregiver for the other. At this time the caring needs can become so overwhelming that there's no time left to look after yourself, and your whole life gets drawn into the overlapping area of your Venn diagram. Of course it's an act of love to be the caregiver, and it does provide emotional satisfaction to know that you're doing all you can (even if, sadly, your partner may not be aware of it). But this is when it becomes particularly important – for your sanity, for your own pleasure, perhaps even ultimately for your life – to keep the non-overlapping part of your Venn diagram healthy. There are often community services available for you. One source I found informative is helpguide.org.[16]

A friend who is both thorough and compassionate noticed that I made no mention, in this third set of circumstances of the Venn diagram's relevance, of paying attention to the care-needing partner's non-overlapping area. Very true. There may be things that can be done to create activities in that area, such as finding others to make home visits, using transportation services for outings, occasional day-care centers for occasional activities – that sort of thing.

DESTINATION

A couple is not just a couple; you're also two different people.

EXERCISE

Create your own Venn diagram. How healthy are its parts? Does it suggest changes or additions to what you came up with in the two previous exercises?

COMPLEMENTARY STAGES ON THE HOHO BUS TOUR

If you're interested, Stage H 72 in Route 1 (exploring happiness and the psychology of Life Two) deals with love and sex in this phase of life.

Take A Breath

It's time to move beyond psychology and happiness and practical day-to-day activities, and consider the financial side too.

But I hope you feel you've achieved a lot already (because you certainly have!), and that this has given you confidence.

START THINKING IN
FINANCIAL TERMS

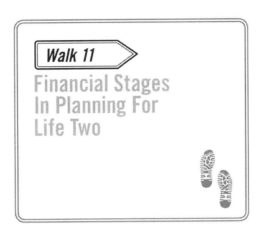

Walk 11

Financial Stages
In Planning For
Life Two

WHERE THE ROUTE TAKES US

Are there any guideposts as to what you should be doing and what you should be thinking about, in connection with retirement, at different stages in your financial life? Let's look at minimum, successful and exceptional standards at five stages.

THE LEARNING

We start with an interview. You may not have checked out Stage H 02 on the Hoho Bus Tour, for which I first interviewed Dan, but that doesn't matter. This is a separate interview. At the time he was afraid I had picked him out because I thought he was unusual, which scared him.

***

Tour Guide [TG]: Welcome back, Dan. I hope you're over the brief attack of nerves you had before Stage H 02.

Dan: Yes, thanks. I've discovered that I'm not nearly as unusual as I feared!

TG: Actually, for this stage you are, in the best way. You mentioned that your son has a job and is living at home, and that your daughter will soon graduate from university. I want to follow up your situation in connection with your son, in particular. Can you remind us what financial arrangements are in place?

Dan: I don't know that I'd glorify the situation with a fancy phrase like "financial arrangements," but I think you mean that he's not paying us rent and instead is contributing half of what his rent would normally be into his company's retirement plan.

TG: That's right. How did that come about? Did you make it a condition?

Dan: Oh no, nothing as formal as that. It all just seemed to be natural.

TG: Natural? You mean everyone does it?

Dan: Oh no, just that it fits into the whole context of our lives.

TG: Can you give us the background that makes it so natural?

Dan: Oh sure. We've always been careful with our money. And I work with a lot of young people, and so many of them don't seem to have a clue about managing their finances. Our family has been used to discussing that sort of thing over dinner when the kids were younger, and from [our son's] behavior he seems to have grown up with good financial sense.

TG: For example?

Dan: Well, like living at home. We love it that he feels comfortable enough to want to do that. We had a brief discussion about ground rules, since he brings friends and girl-friends home, but then that's natural and not new. We like having him and the other young folk around! So it suits us perfectly. What would we do with his room, if he left? We wouldn't rent it out. It would just be waste space, and we wouldn't be better off financially. So he wins and we win too. And half of his financial gain benefits him via more spending money today, and the other half benefits him in the future. He gets it. Did you ever see Sesame Street, the one with Elmo's three jars? "For me, for you, for later." He gets the "for later" bit. It's natural, to him.

TG: Excellent! Anything else?

Dan: Sure. By now he and [our daughter] are pretty literate, financially. So there are so many little things they do automatically. For example, he doesn't buy a fancy coffee every morning. He packs his own lunch every day. (OK, his mother makes it for him.) He doesn't smoke (which makes him healthier too) and only occasionally has a beer, never a binge. His work colleagues say they can't afford to buy a car, they earn so little. But really it's that they spend so much. We brought up our kids to do chores around the house and paid them for it. And half of that money went into our Sesame Street Bank, as we called it – meaning that they gave me the money, and I gave them a receipt for it, and every month I'd give them their bank statement. And I'd then, in front of them, calculate some interest and add it to their total. And that introduced them to the idea of compounding. So they had an incentive to keep the money in the bank! Of course I had to give them much more interest than a bank would, to make it really visible to them, but it was worth it for the education they got!

TG: What an example!

Dan: One more thing, and we didn't even realize we were

teaching them this lesson. It's about borrowing. If they wanted to cash in their savings and add something so that they could buy something they wanted that they couldn't yet afford, we said that was OK, but they'd have to pay the bank interest at the same rate that they were receiving. Oh no, they wouldn't do that! And the attitude seems to have taken, that you should be debt-free. You live on less than you make, so you save. If you have a credit card, it's OK to use it for the convenience of it being a charge card; but if at the end of the month you can't afford to pay it all off, and have to pay interest, then you can't afford whatever you've bought, so don't get in that position. It's a disease that can get out of hand.

TG: I'm curious. If being debt-free is important, did you help them stay that way by paying for their education?

Dan: Yes, we did. That, along with the scholarships. Again, it seemed to [my wife] and me that it was a small price to pay, not just for their formal education but also for an education about life.

TG: And where does that leave you today, personally?

Dan (wryly): Not as well off as we'd like to be. Here I am, at 50, and retirement is something that's starting to have some meaning. Not in a good way. I mean, it's good to think about not having to work, and to do so many things we'd like to do. But where has the time flown? The time to save for retirement, I mean. That's a depressing thought.

TG: I don't mean to pry into your finances, but you and [your wife] own your home, right?

Dan: Right. That has taken most of our cash flow. With today's low interest rates we're paying off the mortgage much faster than we expected. But that also means that I put just enough into my retirement plan to get the full company match, but no additional voluntary contributions.

TG: Actually, you're just arriving at the prime saving years. Paying off your mortgage is just as important to retirement finance as is direct pension saving. And soon, when the mortgage is gone, you too, like your son, can get a double benefit, one for now and one for later. The cash flow that went into your mortgage can be divided into two parts, one to increase your current spending and the rest to save, so that after retirement your added current spending becomes sustainable.

Dan: It's ironic, Sesame Street applies to us too!

TG: Right. What you need now is to see how much income your savings are likely to generate after you retire. You know how much money you've accumulated; now you need to start translating that into monthly income, because you've been used to a monthly budget.

Dan: Yes, I'll do that. Maybe there's a need for "Sesame Street for Pre-Retirees."

***

There really are stages in life. Up to this point I've dealt with psychological stages and transitions. Now I'm going to show that there are financial stages too. Not surprisingly, they're related to the psychological ones, though I'll leave it to you to identify the similarities, if you're inclined to do that.

I don't have financial benchmarks that you should compare yourself against, at each stage. Individual circumstances vary too much for standardized benchmarks. You can judge your progress toward your own retirement goals through your ongoing Personal Funded Ratio calculations (which we'll get to in Walk 18). It doesn't matter whether you're ahead or behind anyone else, let alone some fictitious benchmark person.

Instead, I'll now give you three very rough action criteria at each stage of your financial life. One will be the minimum, one will represent success, and one will be exceptional. As you get nearer to Life Two, the criteria stay the same, but their interpretation changes. What was exceptional in the previous stage now simply represents success, and what represented success now becomes the minimum. But don't take them as rigid guidelines – they're meant as hints to you.

And don't take the dates mentioned in defining the stages too seriously either. Again, they're hints. We're all different, as I keep emphasizing.

Stage 1: The family and career years (up to perhaps 20 years before planned retirement)

The start of your paid working career is a natural starting point for looking at retirement finances. It's hardly a priority, though. Typical priorities at this stage relate to family and career. From a personal perspective you'll want to establish a residential pattern, whether renting or purchasing; keep fit; enjoy life, involving leisure, family and friends.

Nevertheless, minimum retirement-related action steps in this phase are to register for an employment or personal retirement savings plan, undertake to make the minimum contributions permissible, and register for some form of default investment glide path (which we'll look at in more detail in Walk 20). In other words, get started early.

Success at this stage involves saving as much as is necessary to get the maximum "free" match from your employer (if that's the way the plan works), and committing to increases in your contribution rate every time your pay increases.

This isn't easy. You have so many other financial priorities. And you may also be saving indirectly for retirement anyway, via paying down a mortgage.

What's exceptional? Getting into a post-retirement income mindset by doing Personal Funded Ratio calculations, and getting to know enough about your Pillar 1 pension (which we'll look at in Walk 14) to include it in your projections. Yes, this would really be exceptional. In the early years of work it's completely natural to think solely in terms of accumulating wealth towards retirement. Changing from a wealth mindset to an income mindset typically comes much later.

By the way, this may be a good place for me to point you in the direction of a couple of books that I find helpful, but particularly so for those learning in the early stages of saving and investing. One is William Bernstein's *If You Can*,[17] a very short and simple book, aimed specifically at Millennials. The other is by Jonathan Clements, *From Here to Financial Happiness*.[18] It has the same sort of structure I'm planning, some straightforward learning followed by exercises to apply the learning to yourself. I have no connection with either author – I'm simply an admirer of both.

Stage 2: Consolidating the financial base (perhaps 20 to 5 years before planned retirement)

Now you're in your peak earnings phase of your career, and this is when you make the financial transition from paying off debts to accumulating wealth (even though your children's education may make a big claim on your resources). The thing is, if it isn't now, it may be never.

Your social life is still important, as is keeping fit. If you have time (!), this is when you are very valuable as a mentor to young people, because of the experience you have gained.

Being in a retirement savings plan with the maximum free match, with increases in your contribution as your pay increases – these are now the minimum requirements if you want any chance of giving yourself the gift of retirement.

Success? Getting into an income mindset is the only way to identify what you need to do between now and your planned retirement date. Included in what you need to do is a consideration of when you'll move away from the default investment glide path and customize one for yourself.

Exceptional? That's when you're in control of an integrated plan for paying off debt (mortgage and credit cards), financing your children's education, and saving toward retirement.

Stage 3: Getting to maturity (perhaps the 5 years approaching retirement)

Now it's not just a financial priority, it becomes a life priority to establish a plan for graduating from full-time work. And remember that there are three parts to the plan, not just financial but also psychological and practical, identifying the lifestyle you're going to, not just the lifestyle you're going from. We've talked a lot, on previous Walks, about the psychological and practical aspects.

As always, your social activities and keeping fit are important.

Start to identify the experiences that satisfy you and make you happy; explore ways in which you might give something back to society.

At this stage the income mindset and maximizing retirement savings are the minimum financial requirement. It's also time to understand investment risk and set forth on your investment path to retirement, including a customized glide path. And of course Pillar 1 starts to feel like a reality now.

Success? That comes from the mortgage and credit card debt gone, your children's education paid for, your being on target for your retirement financial goal without having to increase contributions. And you're starting to understand longevity (yours alone, plus the combined longevity of you and your partner). And you're considering what to do about post-retirement healthcare and long-term care. We'll talk about all these aspects on later Walks.

What's exceptional? You're ready to start considering your legacy to your children, or even starting to make it available to them in small amounts now. You're making arrangements for a part-time post-graduate career. You're searching for, or may even have found, a financial professional (in which case Walk 22 becomes relevant).

Stage 4: Transition (perhaps the first 3 years of getting into a retirement lifestyle)

Now the priority is to make the transition from full-time work happily, remembering that it's psychologically a new world, and even if you thought you knew what you'd enjoy doing, reality is often different. This is normal, not something to be surprised by or disappointed about.

As always, keep fit. Expand the scope of those social activities that create shared experiences, because typically those are the ones that make you happiest. Experiment with many activities and be honest about what really does satisfy you and make you happy.

The minimum toward retirement finances is now to have registered for your Pillar 1 pension (regardless of when you elect to start drawing it) and for whatever post-retirement healthcare plan you need. Make a decision about long-term care, if you didn't in the previous stage. Find a financial professional. Reassess your financial position (including your Personal Funded Ratio) annually, with your spending pattern starting to establish itself. Make a decision about how you'll deal with longevity risk.

Yes, all of that is the minimum. If not now, when? After all, you're now already living Life Two.

Success comes from everything now being on track, with your estate plans established.

Exceptional? The psychological adjustment is complete – for both you and your partner.

Stage 5: Planning to downsize your lifestyle (perhaps around age 75 or a little later)

Downsizing your lifestyle is a typical phase, and typically it occurs naturally. Getting your financial affairs to match your downsized lifestyle is something that needs to be done consciously. In particular, all financial aspects should now be routine, because that defines your lifestyle too: routine and low-risk.

I have no criteria for you, at this stage. I simply wish you much happiness!

DESTINATION

Think of five stages in your financial life: the first goes up to 20 years before retirement, then the period taking you to 5 years before retirement, then the 5 years taking you to retirement, then the transition into a retirement lifestyle, and finally the point at which you downsize your lifestyle well into retirement. There are different levels of preparedness mentioned for each stage.

EXERCISE

Check out which of the five stages you're in, and evaluate where your preparedness falls in the range from essential through successful to exceptional.

Does this exercise suggest to you that you should be doing something different or something more?

Make a note to revisit this exercise, at a minimum, when you transition to the next financial stage.

COMPLEMENTARY STAGES ON THE HOHO BUS TOUR

If you're interested in a side trip, Stage F 13 in Route 4 (exploring retirement finance) addresses two other considerations that often arise in the first or second stage of your financial life: buying a home, and life insurance.

Walk 20 deals with investment glide paths while you're accumulating assets, and Stage F 12 discusses customizing it.

Stage H 61 in Route 1 (exploring happiness and the psychology of Life Two) tells you a bit more about three possible phases in your post-retirement life.

Walk 12

A Budget Doesn't
Have To Be Detailed
To Be Useful

WHERE THE ROUTE TAKES US

To plan for or evaluate your needs, you must first define them. Financially, this is called budgeting. Sometimes we think that making a budget is a long, complicated process. But for the purpose of setting a financial target, it doesn't have to be.

The learning

When I was young a particular passage in Lewis Carroll's "Alice's Adventures in Wonderland" appealed to my juvenile sense of logic.

> "Would you tell me, please, which way I ought to go from here?" "That depends a good deal on where you want to get to," said the Cat. "I don't much care where – " said Alice. "Then it doesn't matter which way you go," said the Cat.

That came back to me in connection with measuring your progress towards your retirement financial goals. If you don't have a goal, it isn't possible to measure your progress. True, in the previous Walk I described financial stages in terms of activities and mindset, and that's useful as a starting point. But if you have a financial goal, then it's even more informative to be able to measure where you are in relation to the goal.

The passage from Alice is often misquoted as: "If you don't know where you're going, any road will get you there." Yes, but if you don't know where you're going, you probably won't bother to take the first step.

So I think it's useful to have some notion of a spending budget for your entry into Life Two. And if you aren't used to budgeting and the thought scares you, you'll be glad that my point is that a budget doesn't have to be detailed to be useful.

In fact, any number at all is useful for this stage, even if it's just one overall number, simply because it's a number! If all you say is: "I'd like to be able to spend $X a year when my work income stops," that's enough to start calculating how much progress you've made.

Would it make a difference to your mindset if you discovered that you were 50% of the way towards your goal? Or alternatively 100%? Or alternatively 150%? Yes, you would think differently about your progress, depending on which of those turned out to be the measure – isn't that so? In which case, you ought to know which one you're closest to. And, in turn, that's why any starting point at all is useful.

Of course you can refine the starting point in many ways and at many levels of detail, if you want to plan better. But somehow life never quite seems to work out as you've planned. Nevertheless, it's the planning process itself that's the real value, even more than the resulting numbers.

***

How might you choose that first number, $X? And how might you refine it later?

In my case (meaning for my wife and me together, of course), when I first thought about it, the $X I started with was my current salary. It was the gross amount, before taxes and other deductions.

I was still only in my 30s at the time, but I was developing the analysis I called Saving To Afford Retirement (or STAR, since I wanted a cute acronym), which I hoped (ha ha) would earn me money as I applied it to an older clientele. Oh well, that never succeeded, because I had no idea how to reach my prospects. But the thought process helped me personally.

I could equally well have started with my take-home pay, the net amount after salary and deductions.

Would taxation change after retirement? I hadn't a clue. So my first assumption was "no change in taxation," and that deferred that problem for the time being.

The more important adjustment was to allow for all the deductions and other spending that (I hoped) would stop some time before retirement. Of these three were obvious. One was mortgage payments. A second was regular retirement savings. The third was expenditures on children. Assuming all of these would stop at some (unspecified) time and not be necessary to continue after retirement, I deducted them and discovered that my actual ongoing lifestyle required much less than my current income.

Common sense, isn't it? My current lifestyle is measured by what I'm spending on current stuff, not by my total pay packet.

That idea alone tends to make a huge difference, both

psychologically and numerically. And the few clients I used it for got hooked at that point. They had just never thought about it.

***

Wait, won't all these numbers change, every year? Of course. But the process was helpful – and what's more, when a number changed, it was then possible to measure how much the change affected the target. Even a change in the rate of income tax, or in the Pillar 1 benefit, could be interpreted as: "Now I know how I'm affected by that change." (It made the outrage much more specific, to know the impact.)

All sorts of other refinements are possible, such as allowing for an increase in credit card debt or alternatively its elimination. Or expenditures that aren't regular, but you want to budget for them as an average annual amount. Or adding in any new expenditures that you think might start once you're in Life Two. And so on.

I don't know if you've looked at Stage H 44 in the Hoho Bus Tour, in which S and H did their retirement dry run. They started at the other end, with extreme detail, and pretty soon decided that that was unnecessary, and combined a whole lot of items into a simple allowance for each of them that they didn't need to record the details of.

How much detail you'll want to get into will vary with whether you're already running an analysis of your spending or not, what app you're using if that is indeed what you're doing, and so on. Apparently roughly one-third of Americans do so, according to a 2013 Gallup poll.[19] That implies that most don't. And my message to those who don't is just that a tiny start is the most important step of all. The rest is detail.

***

You'll notice that I didn't use rules of thumb like "everyone needs 70% of their pre-retirement income to retire on." For one thing, 40 years ago those rules of thumb didn't exist. But it was also obvious to me that what mattered was my own spending, which might be very different from someone else's, even if we both had the same total pay. And I got at my personal spending, not by creating a detailed budget, but simply by saying "it's whatever is left after all the stuff that will stop, stops."

I was delighted to discover, decades later, that Dr Bonnie-Jeanne MacDonald independently discovered the idea for herself, backed it up with extensive analysis of data from Statistics Canada, and deservedly won global accolades in 2016 for identifying the "living standards replacement rate (LSRR)" as a better measure for evaluating retirement income adequacy than any rules of thumb.[20]

By the way, respected Canadian researchers Malcolm Hamilton and Fred Vettese have also done extensive analysis, and have concluded that most Canadians will live just fine after retirement on something like 50-55% of pre-retirement income – and still save money out of that.[21] So much for traditional rules of thumb.

DESTINATION

Having even a single aggregate number as a spending target is very useful. You can change it and refine it over time, but without it there's no financial goal to measure progress towards.

EXERCISE

Create a budget. The simplest kind has a single number, to represent either the planned spending over a period or the gross (before tax) income over a period. If spending and tax can be separated, that will be useful.

Even better, try to separate spending between what is absolutely essential to your lifestyle and what is desirable but, in a worst case scenario, can be cut (the so-called "nice to have" stuff). In a later Walk, I'm going to ask you if you've done this. If you have, it'll help greatly in understanding your risk attitude. If you haven't ... well, I'll ask you to do that part of the exercise when we get to that Walk.

You'll have guessed by now that this too is something you might want to revisit periodically.

COMPLEMENTARY STAGES ON THE HOHO BUS TOUR

A reminder that Stage H 43 in Route 1 (exploring happiness and the psychology of Life Two) explains why making a plan is important, even though you know it won't work out exactly. And in this Walk 12 I also refer to Stage H 44, about the experience of a couple who did a retirement dry run.

Stage F 21 in Route 4 (exploring retirement finance) could be helpful in persuading you that what's essential and what's nice-to-have is something for you alone to decide, not for society to dictate to you. That stage asks you: what does spending money do for you?

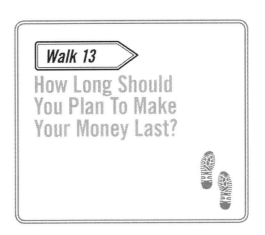

Walk 13

How Long Should
You Plan To Make
Your Money Last?

One very important aspect of a financial plan for Life Two is to have an estimate of how long a time you need to plan for. An estimate of your future longevity (the average length of time that someone of your age and gender in your country can expect to live) will help you to decide on a sensible planning horizon – and that's the ultimate destination of this Walk.

***

If you have an independent estimate of this already, great.

If not, this Walk is for you, as it explains how to use one particular longevity table available on the internet. Another benefit of this table is that it gives you combined estimates for you and your partner, if you have a partner.

In fact, you might want to take this Walk and also take Stage L 12 on the Hoho Bus Tour, if you're in that "independent estimate" place.

The learning

I don't know if you are familiar with what "life expectancy" means. Essentially, it measures the average number of future years that a specified group of people are expected to live.

For example, males at birth. In many countries the average age they're expected to live to might be something like 80 years.

Now consider a different specific group: for example, males in that same country who have survived to age 65. Their average life expectancy might be, let's say, 20 years. That means the average age they're expected to reach would be 85. That's right, the average age they're expected to live to, has gone up from 80. Why? Because this is a different group: it excludes all those who died earlier (meaning, in this case, before age 65); so it's a longer-lived group.

You'll notice that, as you increase the starting age, the average age you're expected to reach, goes up.

Also, half of any specified group (like, males aged 65) will outlive their life expectancy, since it's only an average, not the highest age any member of the group will reach. In other words, of those males aged 65 in our example, half are expected to survive to an age exceeding 85.

For any one person in our example, the actual age he will live to is necessarily uncertain. He may live more than 20 future years, or less than 20 future years. If he wants his financial planning to include a margin of safety, he'll plan for something longer than 20 years.

If any of this surprises you, you should read Stage L 01 on the Hoho Bus Tour as background.

OK, now I'm assuming you're with me, either because you understood the logic behind what I've said, or because you're familiar with what Stage L 01 says.

***

Now let's see what is your life expectancy.

If you already have an independent estimate of it, great. But, despite that, you're not done with the subject. I think it would be useful for you to read on, as you'll need more than just your life expectancy, for planning purposes.

***

In my first draft of this book, I planned a Stage telling you about longevity tables in general. Since then I discovered a very useful one, at http://www.longevityillustrator.org, and so I'll use it as the standard one I refer to, and I'll explain it in this Walk.

But I also recognize that it may not apply to many readers. So in Stage L 12 on the Hoho Bus Tour, I explain how to adapt it to fit your own circumstances. In that way this longevity table should be useful to everyone.

***

The simplest and clearest way to start is to quote from the Welcome message on the website:

"Developed by the American Academy of Actuaries and the Society of Actuaries [in 2016], the Longevity Illustrator is designed to provide you with perspectives on your longevity risk – the uncertainty of how long you and your spouse/partner might live. It does not address your finances, your investments, your earning potential or your anticipated expenses; consult with a financial professional about those aspects of your retirement planning. We invite you to use the Longevity Illustrator to enhance your understanding of the potential risk for outliving your financial resources."[22]

Clearly expressed, and exactly what we need here.

They add:

"The projections shown in the Actuaries Longevity Illustrator are based on mortality tables used by the Social Security Administration in the annual Trustees' Report. There are separate rates for males and females.

"Because mortality rates show a long-standing trend of improving, the Longevity Illustrator is based on the assumption they will continue to improve according to the MP-2015 rates published by the Society of Actuaries. These improvement rates are applied to the 2010 Social Security mortality tables to project mortality rates to future years.

"Additional adjustments are made for health status ranging from 80% to 125% depending on age and for smoker status ranging from 77% to 211% depending on age...

"There are many factors that affect longevity. These include: income, family history, geography, life style, occupation, current medical conditions, and ethnicity. While these all affect longevity, the four factors (age, gender, smoking and health) chosen for this calculator have been shown to account for a significant amount of the individual variations in longevity."[23]

***

As you'll find, the website asks you a (very) few questions about yourself, so that you can get the output you seek.

And then you see the projections. You can print them, change the inputs, and do other useful things. You can see why I like the website so much.

The numbers I'm going to refer to are those called "Planning Horizon" – those are the ones I believe are the most useful, though of course the other numbers can be fascinating in their own right. You can get numbers for yourself alone or for you and your partner. I'll assume you're using the ones for you and your partner. A nice feature is that you can be a male/female partnership, or male/male or female/female.

Let's start with the 50% numbers. These show four things:

Your life expectancy, in years. Remember that half the population outlives their life expectancy. So you have a 50/50 chance of living at least this number of years.

Your partner's life expectancy. Same comment.

Your "joint and last survivor" (or JLS, for short) expectancy (as explained in Hoho Bus Tour Stage L 01). That's the average length of time until the second "estate event" (a term some American insurance agents use, as a euphemism for – how should I say this?

– passing away). So this is the best estimate of the length of time that at least one of you is likely to survive. That's relevant for your planning horizon, because the survivor will need money to live on.

Your "joint" life expectancy, which is the period for which both of you should survive together. Interesting, but not relevant as a planning horizon.

Notice that the numbers are round numbers – no fractions, no decimals. I like this feature. Of course it's possible for techies to go back to the actuaries' original tables and calculate the outputs to as many decimals as one likes. But frankly, who cares? These are all rough estimates, for initial planning purposes, and the decimals are irrelevant. On a subject such as this, using decimals simply demonstrates that you have a sense of humor.

I used one set of inputs (the specifics don't matter), for which these numbers turned out to be 13, 15, 19 and 9, as shown in the diagram below, in the 50% region. (The website uses color, for clarity. In black and white, let's note that the four bars in this case successively mean: male, female, either, both.)

Let's interpret the numbers.

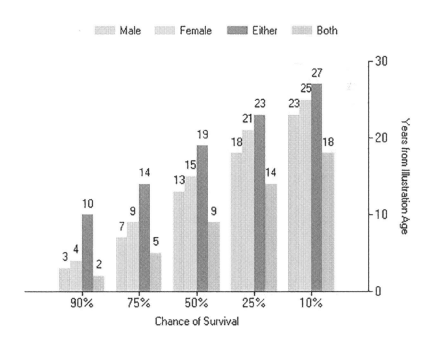

13 and 15 more years are the individual life expectancies of the two partners.

Their JLS expectancy ("either") is 19 years, meaning that that's the best estimate of how long at least one partner of the couple will survive.

Their joint expectancy ("both") is 9 years, meaning the best estimate is that both will be alive together for 9 years.

Interpreting the last two estimates together, it means that the best estimate is that they'll be alive together for the first 9 years, and then the survivor will be alive for a further 10 years.

***

I'm going to ignore the website's 90% and 75% numbers, which I suspect are for curiosity rather than for planning purposes. Let's go to the 25% and 10% numbers.

We start by considering a large group of people of the same age and gender. As we follow them through life, the number remaining will gradually decline. At some point (the 50% numbers above), only half of the original group will be left. Some time later, only one-quarter (25%) of the original group will be left. Later still, only one in every 10 (10%) of the original members will be left. And so on.

The 25% and 10% numbers show the points in time at which 25% and 10% will be left, respectively.

***

I suggest that the relevant 25% number should be your default starting point for your Life Two income planning. That would be 23 years for the partners in my example. (Of course, if the two people were single, the male's 25% number, 18 years, would be the one that's relevant for him, and the female's 25% number, 21 years, would be the relevant one for her.)

Why the 25% number? (Yes, you should challenge me on that point, so that you can decide for yourself whether to go along with the default or to choose something you consider more suitable for your own circumstances. Remember challenging the expert, in Walk 3?)

Suppose you choose the halfway (50%) point as your planning horizon. You may live longer or shorter than that halfway point. They're equally likely. So, if that's your planning horizon, you're as likely to fail to make your money last, as to succeed.

For most people, that's too chancy. Running out of money before you run out of life turns out to be the biggest fear that retirees have. So you'll probably want to make the money last longer than the halfway point.

How about the point at which three-quarters of a group like you have gone, and only one quarter still alive (in other words, the 25% number)? Well, now you're giving yourself three chances out of four, of succeeding to make the money last. That's better.

Or, if you're very cautious, you'll choose the point (the 10% number) at which only one in 10 of a group like you are likely to be alive.

***

Wouldn't you naturally want to be as cautious as possible, with something like this? Not necessarily. Why is that? It's because the longer you plan to make your money last, the less you can draw down each year. That's just common sense, not higher mathematics. If you have $1,000 and want it to last for 20 years, you'll be able to withdraw less each year than if you want the same $1,000 to last for only 10 years.

So there's a trade-off. What you might do, in practice, is two things.

The first is to ask someone to calculate (or maybe do it yourself, via the Personal Funded Ratio calculator in Walk 18) how much you can sustainably draw down from each $1,000 if you plan for the one-quarter or one-tenth points. See how that compares with your desired lifestyle. That could help you decide.

The other is to resolve to adjust, as time advances. For example, this is what my wife and I are doing. We're using the one-quarter (25%) JLS point for planning purposes.

When the first of us goes, that'll require a new calculation, with only the future expectancy of the survivor then being relevant. That will be a shorter horizon, so the sustainable withdrawal will actually increase.

If, as time goes by, we're both still around and in good shape, we'll re-examine our future JLS expectancy at some point, and adjust our planning horizon accordingly. Our hope is that by then we'll have gone from the so-called "go-go" years to the "slow-go" years, and won't need as much money to support our slow-go lifestyle.

Or we'll buy a lifetime income annuity with the balance of our assets, to ensure that we don't outlive our assets.

We'll look at this aspect again in Walk 21, so don't worry about it for now.

Destination

Now you understand and know how to find the 50%, 25% and 10% longevity estimates for you and your partner.

Exercise

Find out what is your expected longevity and the expected "joint and last survivor" longevity for you and your partner (if you have a partner).

Find out the 25% point too (and, if you're curious, the 10% point) for couples like you. You'll need these numbers when the time comes to make and evaluate your financial plan for Life Two.

You don't yet have to decide which point is the one you'll use for your planning horizon. But it might be useful to think about the 50%, 25% and 10% choices, and see if you have an intuitive idea about which one feels most appropriate in your circumstances. Certainly you'll have the chance to reassess it later in the Walking Tour.

Complementary stages on the Hoho Bus Tour

Stage L 01 in Route 3 (exploring longevity) explains the concept

of life expectancy in some detail. Don't be afraid to check it out –
most people misunderstand the concept. And Stage L 12 explains
how to adapt the Longevity Illustrator life table to your situation.

If you're interested in the fact that estimates of longevity seem
to increase over time (as mentioned in one of the quotes from the
Longevity Illustrator website), you could check out Stage L 02.

A reminder that Stage H 61 in Route 1 (exploring happiness
and the psychology of Life Two) goes further into the "go-go" and
"slow-go" phases of Life Two.

Take A Breath

OK, from Walk 12 you have an idea how much money you need each period (year, month, week, whatever) and from Walk 13 an idea of how long the money needs to last. Multiply the two numbers, and that's what you need in aggregate, right? Like $60,000 a year for 30 years, making $1,800,000. Right? Thank goodness, no!

The good news is that it's fine for your assets to be much less than that, for two big reasons. One big reason is that most governments provide an income for citizens or residents of their countries, after some official retirement age. That looks after some of your needs. The other is that typically we invest our financial assets, and hope and expect that there will be a return on that investment that will add considerably more money for Life Two.

Let's now look at those two added sources of money, separately. We'll start with what I'll call your Pillar 1 pension.

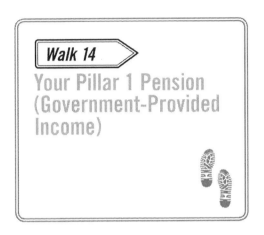

Walk 14

Your Pillar 1 Pension
(Government-Provided
Income)

WHERE THE ROUTE TAKES US

A person's Pillar 1 pension is one of the most misunderstood subjects relating to Life Two. So here are the general principles behind it. Now you won't be prey to the many falsehoods that often surround it.

THE LEARNING

Before we think about your Pillar 1 pension, let me first tell you what it is. And of course you're already ahead of me, and you're wondering how many pillars there are, and what they represent. And why pillars, anyway?

The concept comes from a report by the World Bank in 1994.[24] The idea behind it is that our financial prosperity in retirement can be compared to a structure that is supported by three pillars, each representing income from a particular kind of source.

Pillar 1 is the most general: it's the post-work arrangements for all members of a society. In some countries it's very grandly referred to as a "universal" pension, even though it applies only to that one country. Pillar 3 is the most personalized: it's the set of post-work arrangements arising from an individual's own savings. What's the middle one, Pillar 2? It's the set of arrangements arising from employment: the workplace pension plans, schemes, funds (names vary around the world) that are established for the benefit of employees of an enterprise or for a connected group of enterprises, like all members of a union or all enterprises in an industry.

This classification was so convenient and clear that it has been generally adopted ever since. (Not that we haven't found ways to make it more complicated since then. Don't even ask about Pillar Zero.)

OK, now for a bit of philosophy.

***

It's interesting what each generation takes for granted. The new generation of young ones will take electronics and social media as being like the air they breathe, because they've always been around. I was struck by this thought when thinking about "retirement" – something we all take for granted today.

But look around you. No other species on earth, other than human beings, has been able to arrange for itself the luxury of living happily while not working to scratch out day-to-day survival until death occurs. Of course, a life of luxury has always been there for the few rich ones. But it's only our own last three or four generations that have been able to think of stopping full-time work and living happily thereafter as something for all of us, something we should expect, and plan for. We really are lucky, in that regard. That's why I think of it as a gift rather than a right given to us by nature.

Two kinds of prosperity make the gift possible.

First, there's the general prosperity of the society we live in. It's still not in place everywhere on earth, but where there's general prosperity combined with some social sharing, those societies make a gift of "retirement" to their older citizens.

In some societies it starts earlier than in others. When Bismarck introduced the first government pension in Germany in 1889, it started at age 70. At the time life expectancy at birth was 45, so only a small proportion of the population was expected to benefit from it, and it was not exactly a long future retirement being contemplated. Even in 1935, when Social Security was introduced in the United States, the starting age was 65 and life expectancy at birth was 62, so less than half the population was expected to collect it.

It was only about 60 years ago that societies started to demand a post-work phase of life that would be almost as long as the working phase, and almost as comfortable, but much more leisurely.

In some societies, what is granted is more generous than in others. For example, the US Social Security program started with a limited intention. As President Roosevelt phrased it at the time: "We can never insure one hundred percent of the population against one hundred percent of the hazards and vicissitudes of life, but we have tried to frame a law which will give some measure of protection to the average citizen and to his family against the loss of a job and against poverty-ridden old age."

Today there's starting to be a focus on intergenerational equity, asking whether we're awarding ourselves more than is sustainable for our children – but that's a different question, beyond the scope of this Walk. It's a reminder, though, that we're the beneficiaries of a gift from our society, a gift that can be reduced or taken away. There's a famous US Supreme Court case[25] in which it was confirmed that there's no contractual property right to receive Social Security, and Congress can amend or revise the benefits from time to time. That's another reminder that it's a gift.

***

I have no reading material on government-provided income, which goes by various names. Think of Social Security in the USA, the state pension in the UK, the Dutch AOW pension, the Canada/Quebec Pension Plans and Old Age Security, age pensions around the world, that sort of thing. The reason is that every country has its own system, and telling you about the details in any one country is absolutely useless in every other country.

In fact the entire process varies.

Originally – and this is still how it works in most countries – the government simply added a tax (often called a contribution rather than a tax, but that just disguises its true nature) and used its proceeds to pay some benefit to those who qualified by age and/or years of work or residence in the country. Techies call this system "pay as you go," or PAYG for short, since there is no invested money backing it. Obviously the sustainability of the system improves if there are increasing numbers paying the tax and decreasing numbers collecting the benefits. The trend, though, tends to be in exactly the opposite direction: decreasing numbers of workers paying the tax, and increasing numbers of retirees collecting the benefits. Long-term sustainability, at least at current levels of taxes and benefits, is then clearly in question.

In some countries "funding" has been started, as a sustainable alternative. Chile, in 1981, started this trend. Here each worker's payment is set aside in an account credited to that person, invested over the years, and available at retirement to that person. Australia is another example of a country that now uses this approach. Sweden is an example of a country that sets up "notional" accounts, that is, accounts that exist on paper but are not backed by specific investments. And already you can see how much more variety is feasible!

Also, the amounts required to be paid in, as well as the benefits paid out, vary enormously from country to country. In some countries the benefits are aimed at replacing a large proportion of the average worker's wage. In other countries the benefits are little more than basic subsistence amounts.

All I can tell you as a general statement is that the Pillar 1 pension is a potentially very important source of income, and you should understand how it works in your country. This is an area where you will almost certainly need to seek expertise, which may come from the government itself, from your employer, from a book – whatever. You'll need it to complete the exercise that follows.

***

Let me make an important distinction here. The arrangements in countries like Chile, Australia, Sweden can be considered Pillar 1 pensions, in that they apply to all people there. But for the purposes of our Walks and the related exercises that will enable you to make and evaluate your own arrangements, I think it's important NOT to treat them as Pillar 1, at least in the sense that they specify an accumulation account rather than a specific amount of income.

In other words ... If your Pillar 1 pension is expressed in terms of a specified income, go ahead with the exercise that follows. If it doesn't – if it's specified in terms of an accumulation account – then see if there's a way identified by the government to convert it into an income amount. In that case, once again you can go ahead and treat it as a traditional Pillar 1 pension, using the income amount.

But if all you know is that there's an accumulation account in your name, and there's no official way to convert it into an income, then treat it as if it's a Pillar 2 "defined contribution" or Pillar 3 pension. We'll deal with those in Walk 18.

***

Remember I mentioned two kinds of prosperity that make the gift of Life Two financially feasible?

The second kind of prosperity that makes it feasible is personal prosperity, combined with the means to set aside some of that prosperity while we're working, so that we can have something available for ourselves to draw down, to live on, after we stop working. This becomes a personal gift from ourselves to ourselves, over and above the gift that our society gives us.

Some societies assist this personal process by reducing or deferring taxes for those who demonstrably set aside money for retirement. Much of the rest of the Walking Tour will be concerned with the process of saving money, of investing it, and finally of drawing it down to live on in Life Two. But for our purpose it doesn't matter whether the saving and investing are tax-efficient or not. We talk about that a little bit in Walk 15. I simply say that you should look at all your assets in total.

The more you save personally, the more you'll be able to use the freedom of choice that Life Two represents.

DESTINATION

A happy life after work is a gift made in various ways to ourselves, and it's up to us to use the freedom it gives us.

EXERCISE

Find out about your Pillar 1 pension. As I mentioned during the Walk, you may need to seek an expert's help in answering these questions.

What is the standard age at which it starts?

Is it an income that relates only to you, or does it apply to your partner too?

If it's only to you, does your partner have an independent right to a Pillar 1 income?

Do you have the right to make it commence earlier than the standard age, or alternatively defer its commencement until a later date?

If so, does it become smaller if you start earlier and larger if you start later? By how much?

Is the income guaranteed (at least, until the government

changes the law!) to remain the same each year, or is it guaranteed to increase with (for example) the cost of living, or does it vary according to investment conditions?

The more you can understand how your Pillar 1 pension works, the better you will feel about your personal financial plan for Life Two, since typically this is a very important component of the plan.

And now I'm going to be a little bit sneaky.

I haven't focused at all on any Pillar 2 pension you may have. But now I want you to find out about it. It's particularly important if you have what's called a "defined benefit" pension or if you're a member of a "collective defined contribution" or "target benefit" type of arrangement, because in these designs you have an income coming to you after some date or from some age; and while this is obviously a form of asset for you, its value is typically very hard to discover.

If your Pillar 2 pension arises from a "defined contribution" or "individual account" arrangement, you don't need to check on it just yet. That'll come up in the exercise that follows Walk 18.

But for the Pillar 2 pension arrangements where your benefit is expressed as an income, here are some of the things you can establish. As you can guess, they're very similar to the elements that define your Pillar 1 pension.

What is the standard age at which your Pillar 2 pension starts?

Is it an income that relates only to you, or does it continue to your partner too?

If it's only to you, is there a way to have it continue to your partner, if your partner survives you? Does this survival arrangement decrease the amount of income you will receive?

Do you have the right to make it commence earlier than the standard age, or alternatively defer its commencement until a later date?

If so, does it become smaller if you start earlier and larger if you start later? By how much?

Is the income defined to remain the same each year, or is it meant to increase with (for example) the cost of living, or does it vary according to investment conditions? In all cases, of course, that's assuming there's enough money set aside in the pension fund to back up the stated income – an issue that's beyond the scope of this book.

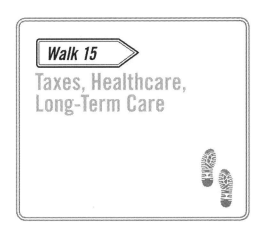

Walk 15

Taxes, Healthcare,
Long-Term Care

WHERE THE ROUTE TAKES US

There are two other extremely important aspects of Life Two that vary greatly across countries. One is the way in which taxation changes, either in Life Two generally or after a certain age. The other is how the country's systems for healthcare and long-term care operate. These are very important aspects, because they potentially involve large amounts of money, so you need to know how they work in your country.

The learning

The US Internal Revenue Service has the following quotation inscribed above the entrance to its headquarters in Washington, DC: "Taxes are what we pay for a civilized society." It's attributed to the Supreme Court Justice Oliver Wendell Holmes, Jr. Mind you, he might not have liked the resulting civilization, because he is also quoted as saying, a couple of years later: "The liberty of the citizen to do as he likes so long as he does not interfere with the liberty of others to do the same ... is interfered with ... by every state or municipal institution which takes his money for purposes thought desirable, whether he likes it or not."

The fact is that we pay taxes. My point here is not that we may not like what our taxes are used for. Instead, my point is the apparently arbitrary way in which taxes are levied. Instead of a few simple rules, tax codes typically consist of multiple volumes characterized by huge complexity. It's as if you are asked to approach the taxing authorities with all your money stuffed into various pockets in the clothes you are wearing, and they say, "From that first pocket we'll take 40%, from the one next to it 20%, you can keep whatever is in that third pocket, from the fourth one 22.5%, from the fifth one..." And so on.

In many countries it's even more complicated than that. If you put more money in one pocket, they'll take away money from a different pocket.

Once you've experienced this, the natural thought is that, before you approach them next time, you should rearrange your money so that they take much less in total. And you discover that finding out how best to do this is very difficult, and whole tribes of people make their living by getting to know the complexities and advising innocent citizens like yourself about how to minimize their taxes. (And then the laws change ... but let's leave it there.)

Taxation makes a significant difference to the proportion of your earnings that the state permits you to keep for yourself, as opposed to for paying for your society's civilization. Of all the financial issues that are involved in planning for Life Two, taxation is typically one of the most important, perhaps even the single most important one.

Think of it this way. You have a dollar. Whether you're allowed to keep 50 cents of it for yourself, or 75 cents, or the whole 100 cents, makes a huge difference to you. (Or if you have one euro, or how many pennies in the pound you can keep, and so on. You get the idea.) Taxation typically has far more impact than the investment arrangements that are made for you.

That example of adding money to one pocket and finding that the government then takes money from a different pocket can be particularly insidious for the lower-paid members of our society. For example, the government may offer supplementary payments to those with very little income. Then, when those recipients earn more income on their own (more money in your earned income pocket), the supplementary payments may be reduced dramatically (they take money out of your supplementary payments pocket). In some countries it may be possible to earn more income in a way that doesn't result in losing the supplementary payments.

I'm not making a moral judgment on whether this is socially desirable or not – I'm just saying that the tax code can be so complex and interactive that adjusting to it could be the most significant financial thing you do.

So you might want to consider getting good tax advice.

You won't find any from me. Not that my goal is to make you a tax expert – that would be inconsistent with my general goal anyway, which is not to give advice but to educate you to the point where you can have an informed conversation with experts. But as regards taxation, I won't even make any attempt at outlining principles.

The reason is the apparently arbitrary nature of tax rules. Ask any country's foremost tax expert to go into another country and use the approaches that work in the first country, and the expert will tell you that the second country requires quite different approaches.

It isn't just the tax rates that differ. Even the principles on which taxes are based differ. Consequently there isn't a universal set of principles that I can tell you about, or even anything close to one. What is tax-exempt in one country is partly taxable in another and fully taxable in a third. Taking money from Pocket A and placing it instead in Pocket B in one country becomes a procedure that should be reversed in a second country, while a third country labels its pockets in a different alphabet altogether.

That's why I have no education to offer you on taxes. All I can say is: the subject is important, don't ignore it, and you might want to seek advice on this issue even if you choose a do-it-yourself approach on other retirement issues.

***

In the same way that there aren't universal principles to apply in connection with taxation, so too with healthcare, meaning how you maintain or improve your health over time. And with long-term care, meaning the need for access to 24-hour nursing care or daily personal support services, typically as one approaches the end of life.

***

All I can do is suggest questions, in the exercise that follows, that might make it easier for you to understand what is available to you.

DESTINATION

The subject of taxation is important. Don't ignore it. You might want to seek advice on this issue even if you choose a do-it-yourself approach on other retirement issues. And as with taxation, the need for healthcare and long-term care can have a significant impact on your finances.

EXERCISE

Find out about taxation and healthcare and long-term care in your country. Typically these are subjects for which it's worthwhile to find experts, even if you have to pay them.

Among the many possible taxation issues that might be worth finding out about are these:

Do you know what proportion of your total income (whether from work, from investments, from retirement drawdowns, whatever) you pay in regular taxes (income tax, capital gains tax, other payments that may not be called taxes but have the same impact – that sort of thing)?

Is your partner taxed independently, or are you taxed as a couple?

Are there reasonably convenient ways of rearranging your financial affairs (the pockets I wrote about in the learning), or even changing the ownership status between you and your partner, to reduce your tax burden?

In particular, are there ways to improve the tax-efficiency of your asset returns without changing the overall structure of your assets (for example, moving some assets from general taxation to tax-favored status)?

In what ways will your tax situation change after you retire? Does it depend on your age? On whether or not you still work part-time? On your partner's work status or income?

Here are some healthcare-related issues. These are all matters that will affect how you spend your money and how much healthcare risk you expose yourself and your family to.

These issues are relevant at all times, but are most likely to be part of what you're thinking about while you're working.

What is it that gives you access to healthcare? Is it a so-called entitlement, legally? If so, does it come from national or state/provincial legislation? Or does it come with your job, or union membership? Or do you have to purchase it from a provider of insurance? Or make some other arrangement?

To the extent that you have access, is it limited geographically? If you are in some other legal jurisdiction when you require healthcare, what conditions and limitations apply? For that matter, do you have the right to seek healthcare in a different jurisdiction and have your source of coverage pay for it?

Is your access time-dependent? Is there, for example, a waiting period before your coverage begins? Is there a time or some age at which your coverage ends? In which case, what are your options at that point?

What are you covered for? Prescription drugs, dental care, eyecare, illness? Are there any exclusions that apply (for example, pre-existing conditions)?

To what extent are you covered? Completely? For all but some deductible amount? For catastrophe only? In other words, what are the limits and conditions?

How much choice are you given in making personal arrangements? For example, can you select your personal physician?

Do you pay for healthcare explicitly (for example, in the form of insurance company premiums) or implicitly (for example, as a part of your taxes)?

Are you permitted to add to your coverage, for example by purchasing supplementary coverage?

Are you permitted to change your coverage?

Does the healthcare system in your country work differently when full-time work stops, or after a certain age?

Typically issues concerning long-term care tend to arise in the post-work years. Here are some of them, again with answers that typically vary from one jurisdiction to another.

Do you have an entitlement to long-term care? Or is it something you have to make your own arrangements for?

How convenient or inconvenient is it to actually get access to long-term care? In other words, if you or your partner ever need long-term care, how might you seek it, and what might it cost?

Who decides whether or not your condition requires long-term care?

Is it possible to receive care in your own home?

If you are moved to a care facility, who pays for it? Or, to put it another way, to what extent do you explicitly pay for usage?

What happens if you can't afford to pay for usage? For example, is there state-provided coverage for the poor? What if your initial ability to pay runs out over time? Can you be forced, for example, to sell your home? If your home is co-owned by one or more family members, can they be forced to sell their shares in your home?

Again, as you can imagine, these are questions to which the answers may have a serious impact on your finances.

You have already covered an amazing amount of ground. You are already extremely well informed. I hope you feel you have come a long, long way since you started on this Walking Tour – because you have. Look around you and smile. Do you think your friends and relatives are as well-informed as you are?

***

Now for the final new topic. It's about investments. The topic may have cropped up as you did the exercises after earlier Walks. Regardless of whether or not it did, this is now where we start to understand the basics: the purpose, the goals, the way you react to a fall in their value – that sort of thing.

Professionals like to tell you how complicated investments are. Well, any subject can get complicated, but we don't need to understand the complications of every subject. And regarding investments, it's actually only necessary to understand a few principles, not legal and tax stuff.

We'll cover that on this part of the Walking Tour, and then help you put everything together in a financial plan that you'll understand.

INVESTMENTS ACTUALLY OFFER SIMPLE CHOICES

Walk 16

Overview Of Investments

WHERE THE ROUTE TAKES US

Understanding investments seems impossible. Who knows where to start? And there are so many kinds of investment. Yet it's absolutely unnecessary to think in those terms. All that's necessary is to understand a couple of very basic things: why people invest, and what sort of general goals they have for their investments.

The learning

Investments are complicated, aren't they? Actually, no more complicated than anything else. Anything gets complicated if you start to explore it in sufficient depth. Investments are no different. It's just that professionals like to tell you how deep and involved and multi-dimensional the subject is. And yet I think that, as with so many other things, the basic principles are relatively easy to understand.

You don't need to know the legal definitions of assets, you don't need to be intimately familiar with investment history, you don't need to know the mathematics of statistical distributions, you don't need to understand long tails or fat tails or other aspects of investment jargon, you don't need to understand taxation, you don't need to know where and how to do trading. Those are informative, but you don't need any of that in order to understand investment principles.

That's my theme here. And so my purpose is to explain the principles in a commonsense non-technical way. No doubt you'll deal with numbers at some stage, but first this will give you a context in which to place the numbers, and then you'll find that their interpretation becomes easy once you understand the context.

***

For completeness, there's one preliminary definition you need, and it couldn't be more fundamental. What's an investment? It's setting aside money today to give to someone (or to some entity) to help conduct an enterprise that you hope will bring you a profit. It's common sense that you'd prefer to spend the money today, and you wouldn't be inclined to set aside money today... unless you had at least a hope that it would grow in the future, via that profit, so you'll probably have even more available to spend in the future. That's the motivation to invest.

That hoped-for future profit could come in many forms. That's what typically gives rise to the jargon name for your investment (the "asset class," as it's called). For example, the amount you hope to get as a profit may be clearly defined in advance (for example, 5% of whatever you invest), in which case the asset will have a name like bills or bonds or fixed interest or fixed income. Or the profit may just be a share of whatever's left after all those "defined in advance" people have been paid, in which case the asset will have a name like stock or equity or shares.

There's no certainty that any enterprise will succeed. But as the global economy expands, the odds ought to be in your favor. (Or you may prefer to restrict your investing to one country or even one enterprise.)

That's it.

***

You're probably familiar with putting money in a bank. The amount is held in your name. Typically, interest may be added from time to time. That's one form of investment.

That's not how you invest in bonds and stocks and more complicated stuff like that. For that, typically you buy some of what you're looking for in investment markets, where the assets are brought to market and sold. More probably, rather than do it yourself, you'll buy into a fund that does the work for you. Funds go under a variety of names, like mutual funds, commingled funds, exchange-traded funds, and so on.

The nice thing is that, particularly in developed markets (as they're called), you can not only buy investments, you can even sell an existing investment to someone else, if you can agree on a price. And if there are lots of willing buyers and sellers, and lots of information about the prospects of a particular enterprise, it won't be difficult to reach agreement on a price that buyers and sellers agree is fair. Of course, since the future is unknowable, some will do better than others at the agreed price – but in the absence of a crystal ball, the prospects favor neither buyer nor seller at the expense of the other.

You'll also find that people hate to take risks, particularly large risks. (Surprised? Of course not!) But some will be willing, at least to some extent. In fact, it makes sense to divide investments into two basic types: safety-oriented (where relative certainty of the outcome is more important than growth prospects) and growth-oriented (much more profit hoped for – but less certain).

You'd think that investments for which the profit (or interest) payable is clearly defined in advance (like bonds) would be clearly safety-oriented, right? That's what they ought to be. And that's what they are, in fact, if you hold them and collect what's promised. Their predictability is an appealing characteristic.

But if you want to trade them, then they're no longer safety-oriented. That's because the price at which you can sell them isn't predictable, but depends instead on how traders in the marketplace view the investment's future prospects – which can vary, even from day to day. And so, what the average non-investment-oriented person thinks of as being safe, is really stuff like bank deposits and similar instruments; and things like "bond funds," which imply constantly changing prices, are considered risky by the average person, because you can't think along the lines of: "I'll need that money in three years' time, and I know what I'll get."

I think that the common-sense average-person perspective is very sensible, and it's what I'm going to use. Something is safety-oriented if the amount you'll get is predictable, on a predictable date, and you intend to collect it on that date; if not, it needs to be considered growth-oriented, because of the uncertainty involved in owning it.

This next bit is a sort of hair-splitting, but I need to say it. The geeks are going to interject here that even things that say exactly what they'll pay out, on exactly what dates, aren't necessarily safe, because the enterprise behind it might fail, or default, and renege on the promise. And the geeks are absolutely right. That's why I won't talk about safe investments, because in that sense, nothing is ever perfectly safe. I'll just call them safety-oriented, recognizing there's an intent but not a guarantee.

How you decide to split your investments between safety-oriented and growth-oriented is a fundamental question. And there's no one-size-fits-all right answer. It'll depend partly on your financial position and partly on psychological considerations.

Yes, we're going to cover all that territory, coming up.

***

There's one final distinction I want to make. It concerns what's called "liquidity." Liquid assets are those you can convert to cash pretty quickly and with little or no decrease in value when you convert them to cash. For example, money in a bank account. You can get your hands on it right away, and you know how much you'll get. In contrast, illiquid assets are those that typically take time to get your hands on, and the process of converting them to cash may result in a decrease in their value. For example, your home, or a boat – that sort of thing. The degree of illiquidity can obviously vary from asset to asset.

The main reason I bring this to your attention is that, for many people, their illiquid assets have an emotional significance, and they may want to leave them to someone without having to go through the process of selling them. And so these people may want to see if they can live happily through Life Two without having to contemplate selling their illiquid assets. And for those who own their home, typically their home is their biggest asset.

We see later, after Walk 18, whether or not you need your illiquid assets for your Life Two lifestyle.

DESTINATION

Investing means setting aside money today in the hope that it will produce more in the future. There are basically two kinds of investment: safety-oriented (where relative certainty of the outcome is more important than growth prospects) and growth-oriented (much more profit hoped for – but less certain). And some investments are liquid, and others less so.

EXERCISE

Now that you understand the simple principles of investing, check your "portfolio" of assets, as the totality of what you own is often called.

Include all your assets, not just the stuff specifically earmarked or named for retirement. After all, everything you own can be used to support your lifestyle in Life Two. It may be that the so-called retirement assets get favorable tax treatment, in which case that's great; but that doesn't mean that (for example) your home and your bank accounts aren't assets too. So, include everything.

Can you classify your assets by whether they're safety-oriented or growth-oriented? Note that some will be riskier than others, within the growth-seeking category. That doesn't matter for this exercise: growth-seeking is growth-seeking.

What proportion of the total is safety-oriented? What proportion is growth-seeking?

Do you have any instinctive reaction as you make this distinction? Do you feel you ought to have more in safety-oriented assets? Or less? Why? What gives rise to that feeling? It's typically very difficult to explain how you feel or decide how you ought to feel. That's why we'll explore that issue in our next Walk.

There's one more distinction I want you to make, in this exercise. I want you to classify your assets in another way too: by whether they're liquid or illiquid.

What proportion of the total is illiquid?

Complementary stages on the Hoho Bus Tour

If this is too basic for you, or if you want to go further, there are four stages in Route 2 (exploring investment) that should be fun to read. Stage I 11 sets out four commonsense but profound investment principles. Stage I 12 then suggests how to think about different kinds of investments. The stages use the analogy of a casino or playing cards or tossing a coin to teach the principles.

Stage I 21 gets into real life detail, examining and drawing conclusions from actual historical patterns of investment returns. And, as a cautionary note, Stage I 22 is a reminder that sometimes bad things happen for long periods.

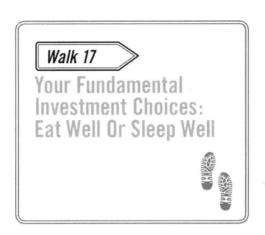

Walk 17

Your Fundamental
Investment Choices:
Eat Well Or Sleep Well

WHERE THE ROUTE TAKES US

You have two fundamental investment options: seek safety, or seek growth. Most of us want some of each, rather just choosing one and rejecting the other. What mixture do you want? On this Walk we'll see that the mixture that best suits you depends on how much you want to eat well and how much you want to sleep well. It really is as basic as that.

The learning

How much investment risk can you tolerate? That's what this stage is all about.

Many investment practitioners and websites have created risk tolerance questionnaires. Depending on the answers you give to the questions in them, you end up categorized in a particular way (such as "conservative" or "moderately aggressive" or whatever) and assigned a particular allocation of different types of assets.

I've tried many of these questionnaires, and I've found them unhelpful. Partly it's because their generic questions are often far removed from any person's own situation. But also, they're questions related to investments, and frankly (even as someone whose career has been spent in that field) I think that's virtually irrelevant. Most of us don't have a gut feeling for whether a bad investment outcome is really bad or just a bit bad. But if you translate that bad investment outcome into the impact it has on our lifestyle, then yes, we can tell whether it's really bad or just a bit bad.

And that's my point. Investing isn't an end in itself. It's only a means to an end. It's a way to make our assets grow, so that we can live the lifestyle we desire in Life Two. We should discuss risk in terms of the impact it has on your goals, on your desired lifestyle. That's the language to use, not investment language.

In life we can think generally of two kinds of goals. At one extreme we want to make sure that we survive, otherwise nothing else matters. At the other extreme we want to thrive, to be fulfilled, to be happy. At different times, as our circumstances change, one goal can become more important than the other, for the time being. But in general, those represent the two extremes.

It's the same with investment. At times when survival is the dominant goal, we seek investment safety. And when thriving is what we aim for, the corresponding investment goal is growth. First lock in safety; then seek growth with the rest.

***

That commonsense way of looking at life should also reassure you that there's no right or wrong answer to investment risk tolerance. It's just a question of what you're most comfortable with – or perhaps least uncomfortable, because even though you may not be comfortable with any of the available choices, you still have to choose one.

In fact, another way to express your essential choice is to ask where you place yourself in another formulations of extreme goals: to eat well and to sleep well. I remember saying this to a group of pension fund participants, and it drew a round of nervous laughter. Surely that has nothing to do with investing! Surely it's too simple a characterization! No, it's accurate and not over-simplified.

Typically, those who are at the "eat well" end of the spectrum have a long-term focus. They want to accumulate enough wealth to be able, as the goal states, to eat well in Life Two, to live their desired lifestyle to the fullest extent. They know, because they understand investment principles, that most of that wealth will come from the investment return, and that, in seeking a high return over the long term, they must endure a high degree of short-term uncertainty and volatility. (This shouldn't surprise you. The notion that an asset can bring a high return with very little risk is simply too good to be true – common sense.) But these growth-seekers are willing to endure that short-term uncertainty, even though they also know that there is no guarantee that they will succeed in getting the growth they desire.

Those at the "sleep well" end of the spectrum may also share a long-term focus, but they can't live day to day with that kind of uncertainty. They can't sleep at night if their future is profoundly uncertain and seems to vary in its prospects from day to day, with every gyration of the markets. So, even though they realize that cutting back on risk also means cutting back on opportunity, they choose to live with low risk.

The choices are at opposite ends of the spectrum, because pursuing the goal of eating well compromises sleep.

***

Which end of the spectrum is more sensible? The answer is: they are both sensible. Being sensible isn't a matter of seeing who ends up with the most money, or who sleeps most soundly. It's not a contest. It's a matter of making a choice you can live with. And people are different, it's as simple as that.

Most of us are probably somewhere between the ends of the spectrum. We're not entirely opposed to taking some risk. Equally, we're not willing to take enormous risk. We do know, though, that the biggest fear of retirees, according to surveys, is outliving their assets. Sleeping well is therefore the higher priority. That's entirely consistent with ensuring that you survive before you try to thrive.

What determines a sensible place in the spectrum?

Essentially, there are two kinds of considerations. One is financial and one is psychological. We'll examine them in Walk 19, right after (in Walk 18) getting a first estimate of how well placed you are, comparing the income you need for your desired lifestyle, against the income you're likely to have available.

DESTINATION

How much safety and how much growth should you seek? That depends on how you balance your goals of eating well and sleeping well.

EXERCISE

Go back to the answers you gave, when you did the exercise at the end of the previous Walk.

When you think in terms of eating well and sleeping well, does your allocation of assets between growth-seeking and safety-seeking seem intuitively appropriate to you?

It's OK if you can't translate your risk attitude into an appropriate mixture of the two kinds of goals. Frankly, there's no formula to do so. Even for mathematicians, intuition plays a large part! So in Walk 19 we'll go further into the psychology of facing risk; and before that, in Walk 18, we'll see how well you've "funded" your desired Life Two lifestyle.

COMPLEMENTARY STAGES ON THE HOHO BUS TOUR

Stage F 03 in Route 4 (exploring retirement finance) tells us why investing is only a means to an end, not an end in itself.

Stage F 02 shows how, over a lifetime, typically the vast majority of what you end up with comes not from money you set aside initially, but from investment returns over the years.

Stage I 21 in Route 2 (exploring investment) is relevant again, showing that high returns over the long term are associated with high uncertainty and volatility in the short term.

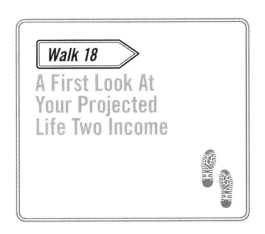

Walk 18

A First Look At
Your Projected
Life Two Income

WHERE THE ROUTE TAKES US

In this Walk we'll focus on two questions. One is whether you're in danger of outliving your assets, if you live your desired lifestyle in Life Two. If the answer is yes, we'll then look further at the second question: how much of your desired lifestyle is likely to be sustainable, and what you might be able to do to improve the situation.

The learning

OK, it's time to make a first estimate of the income you'll get throughout Life Two from your total assets.

Why only a first estimate? Because there are always things you can do to attempt to improve the situation, if you don't like the answer.

If you are still in Life One, you have many possible dials to turn:

- You can save more.
- You can retire later.
- You can take more investment risk.
- You can cut from the "nice to have" part of your hoped-for lifestyle budget.

The first two will undoubtedly reduce or eliminate the gap between the income you'd like and the income that is likely. The third, of course, is a hopeful step towards success; no, it's more than a hope, it's an expectation – but it isn't certain. All these three dials aim to stretch your income to bring you closer to your goal. The fourth brings your goal closer to where you're likely to be.

If you're already in Life Two, the first two dials are no longer available to turn.

Because this is so important to defining your lifestyle, it's worthwhile to make that first estimate, so you'll have an initial idea of where you stand.

***

The tool for making the estimate is my Personal Funded Ratio (PFR) calculator, on the website, where it has its own section, headed Calculator at the top of the first page. The calculator has five stages on the Hoho Bus Tour to describe all the things you can do with it, and how. That's beyond our scope on this Walk. Here we'll just examine what it means, and how to use it for two specific calculations.

***

First, what PFR means.

As its name states, it's a ratio. So it compares two things. It compares the income you're likely to have with the income you need for your desired lifestyle. If the ratio exceeds 100%, that's good, implying that you have more than enough. If it's below 100%, action is indicated, because it implies that you don't have enough. Accumulating assets to meet your needs is called "funding" in the jargon of pensions, so this is your "funded ratio." And since it applies to you, it's your "personal funded ratio." The concept is as basic as that.

***

Obviously, we now need to project the income you need, and the income you're likely to have available. Fortunately, without realizing it you've already gathered almost all the information required.

By the way, the calculator stores nothing on the website (for your security), and you can't download it, so it may be sensible to print out the results when you do your calculations, as a record of the results. Before you leave the calculator you can change the inputs if you want to test something different, and after leaving it you can always enter new information and start again.

Everything from this point on is really the start of an extended Exercise associated with this Walk.

***

Enter the relevant personal information, and the number of years to your planned retirement. Of course the years will be zero if you're already in Life Two.

In this Walk I'm going to consider only the "best estimate basis," so I'll ignore anything to do with the "locked-in basis." Check out the complementary stages on the Hoho Bus Tour if you're interested in the locked-in basis.

As an example, I'm going to use Alain and Amélie's information, from Stage F26 on the Hoho Bus Tour. It's mentioned in the Complementary Stages at the end of this Walk. I'll call them A&A.

If you look at Stage F26, you'll see they weren't sure about many of the numbers.

Right now A&A are both 40 years old, and they're calculating their PFR if they retire in 25 years.

For the years of income needed, enter the 25% number from Walk 13 in the "best estimate basis."

For A&A, this is 32 years.

Enter your target gross annual income, from Walk 12. It might be interesting to enter your current gross income too, to see what proportion of your current gross income is required to support your desired Life Two lifestyle.

For A&A, these numbers are $115,000 for gross annual income and $80,000 for target annual income.

And that's all you need, to define your target financial situation.

**

Now let's see how much annual income you're likely to be able to sustain.

From Walk 14, enter your estimated Pillar 1 and Pillar 2 "defined benefit" pensions.

For A&A, those are $30,000 and $0.

That's the base. Now we have to see how much income you can sustainably generate from your personal assets (Pillar 3, and also Pillar 2 "defined contribution" or "individual account").

We'll start with your current assets, from Walk 16. There I suggested dividing them between liquid assets and illiquid assets. That's because you may own your home – indeed, for most people who own their home it's often their biggest asset – and you may not want to use it to generate income for Life Two. I suggest you include it here anyway. You'll see why in a moment.

For A&A, those numbers are $150,000 and $300,000 respectively.

OK, those are your current assets. If you're still saving money towards retirement, you'll also want to estimate the income your future savings are likely to generate. That requires different information, so for now, hit "choose a calculator" and select "your personal funded ratio."

On the new page, enter the amount of future annual savings. These are amounts that will increase your accumulated assets, but don't include anything going towards your Pillar 1 or Pillar 2 "defined benefit" pensions which we took into account in Walk 14, as we've already allowed for these. So, these future savings are typically amounts contributed by you and your employer to a "defined contribution" arrangement, or any additional savings you're making on your own.

If you're already in Life Two, or aren't making any more savings, enter 0 here. If the calculator won't accept 0, enter 1 (which doesn't affect the results).

For A&A, their number is $9,200.

How about those "assumed annual real returns" before and after retirement? For our first estimate, don't worry about those inputs. For the "best estimate basis," input 2% before retirement and 1% after retirement. (A&A used 3.5% before and 1% after retirement.) I'll explain all this stuff later on this Walk. For now, let's just get the projected income.

So, now you hit "calculate."

***

And here are your results!

Never mind the target assets you require, or the projected assets. Just look at the projected funded ratios. They tell you what proportion of your desired lifestyle is likely to be sustainable, and which assets sustain it.

Ignore the locked-in basis. Check out the best estimate basis.

The total best estimate funded ratio deals with the first of the two calculations I mentioned at the start. If it exceeds 100%, the chances are that you can sustain your desired lifestyle for the time horizon selected. Nothing is certain, of course, because we're hoping we'll make "real" returns of 2% a year before retirement and 1% a year after retirement, and those aren't certain. But anything over 100% is an encouraging start.

You'll see that it's quite simple to see the extent to which different sources (Pillar 1, Pillar 2, current liquid assets, current illiquid assets, future savings) contribute to your total funded ratio.

Here's what the results were for A&A:

Your projected funded ratios	
Best estimate basis	
Pillar 1	38%
Pillar 2	0%
From current liquid assets	16%
From current illiquid assets	32%
From future savings	17%
Total best estimate funded ratio	103%

***

Now let me take the discussion further by identifying three possible sets of results.

Over 100% without illiquid assets. This implies that it's a reasonable expectation that you'll be able to life your desired lifestyle, without having to generate income from your illiquid assets. A highly desirable projection! (Note that A&A aren't there. Excluding their 32% from illiquid assets would have produced a total best estimate funded ratio of only 71%.)

Over 100% with illiquid assets. This also implies that it's a reasonable expectation that you'll be able to live your desired lifestyle, but only if you can generate the indicated income from your illiquid assets. And the indicated illiquid assets imply selling your home. An uncomfortable projection, typically. But remember that you have those dials you can turn (see the start of this Walk) to bridge the gap. (This is where A&A are, at 103% including illiquid assets.)

Under 100% with illiquid assets. This is the most uncomfortable projection outcome. It implies that it's unreasonable to expect your assets to support your desired lifestyle throughout your life, even if you use your illiquid assets towards that end. In turn, it implies a strong need for action via turning the dials.

Whatever the projected outcome, you might want to print the results, to save your base case. Other useful calculations follow, in the Exercise.

***

Notice that, in the "best estimate basis," there's an apparent precision in the projected numbers. In reality, that's just not so, and it's important to understand why.

For one thing, we don't know the future, so an estimate is just that – an estimate. I call it a "best estimate" because that's the focus, but the operative word here is "estimate" rather than "best."

Another reason is that some inputs are more difficult than others to obtain, so let's not worry too much about precision in every input. Let's get a rough estimate first, and then see which inputs have the biggest effect, and consider refining those inputs in a follow-up calculation. It's preferable, I would think, to know whether you're 75% or 100% or 150% funded, quickly, than spend hours or days tracking down precise numbers that may have no more than a 5% impact. (As you'll see if you check out Stage F27 on the Hoho Bus Tour, A&A promptly did a number of other calculations.)

Also, the projection takes no account of the investment risk involved. By this I mean that the outcome could be much better – or, depressingly, it could be much worse. Typically we're pleased if it's better than we projected, and that's fine. But also, typically we feel really bad if it's worse, and that's serious. So nobody should make a decision without first considering, not only the likely outcome, but also a "bad case" outcome. This is where your "risk tolerance," as it's called, becomes relevant, an important part of your education that we'll deal with on the next Walk.

For now, let's base the Exercise on the projections you've just made.

***

I should mention that all calculations are done in what economists call "real" terms, that is, in terms of purchasing power. That means there's no need for a separate projection of inflation. Express your spending needs in terms of what they cost today. Then, we'll express the investment returns in terms of their excess over inflation. For example, a 4% "real" annual return implies that, whatever inflation may be in the future, the investment return each year will be 4% higher.

More on the real returns in the Exercise that follow.

***

Let me add a note. There are numerous calculators available, from financial professionals and on the internet. Many are far superior to the PFR calculator here, taking into account all kinds of variations and being customizable to the nth degree. By all means use one of them instead. Just make sure that you actually perform the calculations mentioned on this Walk, because those are the ones for which I've discussed how to interpret the results.

EXERCISE

If your total best estimate funded ratio exceeds 100% without illiquid assets, the first indication is that your Life Two income should be adequate to support your desired lifestyle for the remainder of your (and your partner's) life, without touching your home.

If not, consider what you want to do about your illiquid assets. Decide whether you want to go with one of the approaches suggested in Stage F 72 on the Hoho Bus Tour.

You can also explore the dials listed at the start.

If you're still in Life One, you can use the PFR calculator to calculate the annual savings, or the annual real returns, required to reach your target.

***

Let me, at this point, help you interpret the real returns, by telling you how I interpret them when thinking about my wife and myself.

I use 0% as a reasonable safety-oriented annual real return, and 4% as a reasonable growth-oriented annual real return.

So you can now tell that, in using 2% for pre-retirement real returns, the projections implicitly place you 50% in safety-oriented assets and 50% in growth-seeking assets, while 1% for post-retirement returns imply 75% in safety-oriented assets and 25% in growth-oriented assets.

Next, when you see what real returns are necessary for you to reach your target, you can see what's the implied mixture of safety-oriented and growth-seeking assets. My strong warning to you is that, if the necessary real annual returns are close to or exceed 4%, you're probably reaching for the moon.

***

Another calculation is that you can change the number of years to your projected retirement date – in which case, remember to change the corresponding 25% longevity number too, and probably also the Pillar 1 and Pillar 2 pensions. Typically, this is the dial that has the greatest impact on the projections.

If all of these approaches still leave you short of where you want to be, then all I can suggest is that, realistically, you need to go back to your desired lifestyle and cut back on the "nice to have" elements. There's no magic wand to wave, to make everything come right.

Finally, if you're already in Life Two, you can calculate the annual real returns required to reach your target, and you can also realistically see where you want to cut back on the "nice to have" elements.

***

At this point you have at least a first estimate of your likely Life

Two annual income, as well as a revision of the budget you created after Walk 12.

COMPLEMENTARY STAGES ON THE HOHO BUS TOUR

Stages F23 – F 27 in Route 4 (exploring retirement finance) explain the PFR and the calculator in great detail, including a discussion of what the locked-in basis means, as well as taking you through a case study in which a couple (A&A) do their own calculations and then start to explore other possibilities if they were to turn some of the dials available to them.

Stage F 72 in Route 4 explains four ways to generate income from the home.

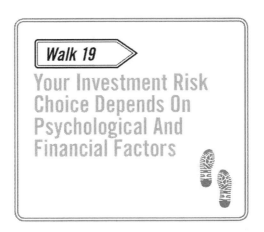

Walk 19

Your Investment Risk Choice Depends On Psychological And Financial Factors

WHERE THE ROUTE TAKES US

How do you decide between the ends of the risk spectrum? Well, your choice depends on both psychological and financial considerations. The financial considerations are to calculate (have an expert calculate?) what effect it has on your lifestyle if your assets fall by 10%, 20%, whatever. The psychological factors have to do with how you'd react to that sort of lifestyle impact. Together, the answers enable you to make a decision on your attitude to risk.

THE LEARNING

Eat well or sleep well? Most of us are probably somewhere between the ends of the spectrum. We're not entirely risk-averse. Equally, we're not willing to take enormous risk. What determines a sensible place in the spectrum?

Essentially, there are two kinds of considerations. One is financial and one is psychological.

**

The financial aspect has to do with a comparison between your goals and your current situation. You can explore how much of a difference it makes if you vary the inputs in projecting your future income, something you might have done after Walk 18. That can give you some idea of the amount of risk you need to take in pursuing your goals – which for many people may be more than the risk they're willing to take. Whatever the outcome of your exploration, it's always helpful to look at this aspect long before you retire. Remember what we discussed in Walk 11, where we looked at minimum, successful and exceptional standards to evaluate what you're thinking about and doing at various stages of your life.

Well, it's the same financial projection exercise after retirement too, even though at this stage you no longer have the benefit of postponing retirement as one of the dials you can turn, as we just discussed on Walk 18.

After the Exercise that followed Walk 18, you have a (possibly new) budget, divided (as before) between expenditures that you consider essential – things you couldn't give up under any circumstances, no matter how bad – and things that you consider nice to have, that you might have to give up if things went sour financially.

Now the next thing to do is to estimate the effect that different levels of investment risk might have on your budget. For example:

if your assets fall in value by 10%, what spending might you have to cut?

***

It's important to realize that you don't necessarily have to cut 10% from your spending, in response to a 10% fall in asset value. This is a fundamental point, so let me explain why. There are three aspects to the relationship between volatility of asset value and volatility of spending, all of which help insulate you, at least temporarily, from the full impact of a fall in asset value.

The first aspect arises if you set up a contingency reserve. In life, you never know what sudden unforeseen expenditures may be necessary. Many people therefore set aside some money "just in case." Financial professionals suggest that, while you're working, a reserve of six months of spending is a good idea. In Life Two, something like 2% of your total assets might be an equivalent rule of thumb. If you do this, of course, you shouldn't use that 2% contingency reserve (or whatever amount you feel you can set aside) in your calculations with the PFR calculator in Walk 18. You should reduce the assets aimed at generating income by that contingency reserve.

The thing is that this contingency reserve can also be used to cushion your spending, if the value of your remaining assets falls. So it isn't absolutely essential to cut your spending right away.

The second aspect is that, each year or each month (or whatever is the period you use for regular drawdowns from your assets for spending), you can use safety-oriented assets for drawdown purposes. That's a big reason – probably the main reason – why you have safety-oriented assets at all in Life Two. It's to provide a source for drawdowns that isn't subject to the same sort of fluctuations in value that your growth-seeking assets inevitably are subject to. And again, it means that you can ride out a fall in total asset value without having to draw down any less or therefore spend any less.

The more you have in safety-oriented assets, the longer the downturn in asset value you can endure in this way. For example, if you have five years' worth of drawdowns in safety-oriented assets, you can give the growth-seeking assets that have fallen in value five years to recover, before you need to cash in anything from that source. Of course, the more you have in safety-oriented assets, the lower your long-term investment return is likely to be, and so the lower is your likely rate of sustainable drawdown. So it's a trade-off: higher drawdowns are associated with less protection against falls in value, lower drawdowns give you greater protection.

The big question is, will the fall in asset value be permanent or will it be temporary? History says that it'll most probably be temporary, and that recovery will come about. That's called "mean reversion," in investment jargon: that fact that (at least so far!) investment returns get back to a sort of long-run normal level eventually.

The thing about risk, of course, is that mean reversion isn't guaranteed. And even if asset values do revert to their previous level, there's no saying how long it'll take before that happens. Nevertheless, your safety-oriented assets buy you time, hoping that values will recover before you run out of safety-oriented assets and are forced to start selling those fallen growth-seeking assets to spend from.

Anyway, my point is that spending drawdowns don't have to respond immediately to falls in asset value.

The third aspect is that your spending doesn't have to be linked immediately and fully to your drawdown. You might, for example, reduce your spending partially in response to a fall in asset value, just in case mean reversion doesn't occur or takes longer than your safety-oriented assets give you protection for. And if, over time, mean reversion still isn't happening, you might keep making cuts in spending gradually. The idea is that you shouldn't wait for your safety-oriented assets to run out completely before you cut spending; that could be a great shock, so get there gradually.

All of this tends to be the sort of thing that might be worth discussing with a financial professional, particularly implementing a strategy that smooths withdrawals and spending. It goes beyond the scope of this Walk. For now, let me simply sum up the financial side by saying that there are three layers of insulating spending from the effects of a fall in asset value:

- An explicit contingency reserve;
- The drawdown can be less volatile than the asset fluctuations;
- Spending can be less volatile than the drawdowns.

***

It can be very complex to set up and maintain investment arrangements with a structure that enables you to invoke this degree of insulation between falls in asset value and reductions in spending. If you are struggling with understanding this, here's the overall message: there are ways to defer the impact of asset value falls on spending.

I should add, for completeness, that it makes just as much sense to do something similar if asset values rise suddenly. In other words, don't raise your drawdown or spending to match the rise. Do it gradually, if at all, because mean reversion implies that a fall to some long-run normal level is likely.

***

The psychological aspect of risk is entirely subjective. Essentially, it is about saying in advance whether some pattern of outcomes will cause you to lose so much sleep that you reject living with that scenario. And there are two kinds of bad outcomes, one that takes place in the short term (think of this as the next year or two), and one that takes place in the long term.

The chances are that if you discuss this with financial professionals, they will talk to you solely in terms of the short term. They'll use phrases like "how bumpy a ride you can live with." Yes, that is relevant, if you're the sort who loses sleep every time your investments lose value. Actually, most of us are like that, at least to some extent. We're afraid – particularly because we have no way of telling what will be the practical impact on our lifestyle, and so we fear the worst.

The way around that fear is to confront it soberly. You might, for example, make an estimate of the impact that a fall of (say) 10% (or 20%, or whatever – perhaps a whole series of estimates) is likely to have on your lifestyle. You may find (at least, that's an outcome to be hoped for!) that the lifestyle impact is far less than you feared, particularly if you or your financial professional can set up the insulating mechanisms I've just described. In other words, that a 10% (or 20%, or whatever) fall in the value of your assets results in a substantially lower percentage reduction in your lifestyle income.

Even if that happens, you may still feel that asset value fluctuations are something you can't sleep with. Fair enough. Now you know that your psychological risk tolerance is low, and you can make your choices accordingly. But if the education that comes from making lifestyle projections makes you tolerate a possible asset value fall more easily, then the education has given you resilience, and has helped you increase your tolerance for short-term volatility.

**

What you're really after is some idea of what may be the long-term impact on your lifestyle, even if you can sleep through short-term asset volatility. This long-term impact, in fact, comes not as a consequence of short-term volatility, but from long-term growth not being as high as you hoped for. For example, the 4% assumption for real annual returns on growth-seeking assets (the basis I use for the PFR calculator in Walk 18) doesn't materialize over the long term.

The difference goes beyond the scope of this Walk. It is explained in Stage T 01 on the Trail for Enthusiasts, distinguishing between "deep risk" and "shallow risk," a distinction you may have to educate your financial professional about, because many behave as if they have not come across it.

Briefly, there is no way around this. If economic growth around the world is lower than is widely and generally expected, the world will suffer. You will be part of it. It may help that you're aware of the possibility, and have considered in advance at least some downward possibility. If you or your financial professional can project (for example, by using the PFR calculator) the impact of a lower long-term annual real return than 4% from growth-seeking assets, you can go through a similar set of considerations in seeing what it does financially to your sustainable income, and how you'd feel psychologically about it.

**

Two final comments.

One is that most people have a nervous first reaction to being asked whether they would rather eat well or sleep well. "Can't we do both (ha, ha)?" And the answer is: yes, it may be possible. Guaranteeing both isn't possible if your Personal Funded Ratio is below 100% using the locked-in basis in Walk 18 (which goes beyond the scope of the Walking Tour). But the arrangements mentioned in this Walk are designed to aim at achieving both ends of the spectrum at least for a period of time, while expressing risk in terms of your retirement income rather than in investment terms.

The other closing comment is to remind you that it's possible to be too relaxed about the prospect of bearing risk. The thing is that risk, until it occurs, is only an intellectual concept. Yes, things may turn out worse than you hope for. The reality is almost certainly more painful than the concept. I'll cite here (as I do in Stage H 22 in Route 1 on the Hoho Bus Tour) a wise quote from a friend of mine who said, after the global financial crisis, that we discovered that "Risk has a friend called Pain." And the reality of Pain is going to be worse than the concept of Risk.

That reality tends to create a different set of emotions when asset prices take a dive. You tend to be frightened rather than calm and rational. The media will be preaching gloom and doom, telling you that the market hasn't bottomed yet (no matter whether, in retrospect, it has or not). You may be tempted to bail out of the market. Only Warren Buffett will be on your side, reminding you that it's a good time to buy.

Under those circumstances, it will be good to have done some simulations about what will be the effect on your lifestyle, because that's the only reality that matters. It'll help you steel yourself in the sure knowledge that your risk tolerance will be tested one day.

DESTINATION

Your risk tolerance depends partly on psychological and partly on financial factors. When considering your risk tolerance, think not in terms of how you react to a fall in market prices – which is likely to be highly emotional – but to how you react to the impact it has on your spending potential – which is a much more sober set of considerations, and which may not be as large a fall.

EXERCISE

Apply these concepts to yourself – and to your partner, whose reactions may be different. (If they are different, you may need to look at Stage I 33 on the Hoho Bus Tour on how to reconcile those differences.)

If your financial assets fall by (say) 10%, does that affect your Pillar 1 pension too, or is that in itself a separate source of stability and safety?

How much of your spending would need to be cut after a 10% fall?

Does that affect only your nice-to-have spending (see the Exercise after Walk 12, on budgeting), or does it cut into your essential spending?

How about a 20% fall? How would that make you feel?

Are you aware (or has your financial professional made you aware) of ways to cushion the impact of a fall in asset value, as described on this Walk?

Does all of this help you to decide how much of a drop you can tolerate, both financially and psychologically?

Once you decide, then your financial professional can translate your reactions into an investment plan.

Finally, when you've decided how much risk you can tolerate: have you ever experienced that sort of fall before, and demonstrated psychological resilience? That's the point made at the end of this Walk. If you have indeed demonstrated risk resilience, make sure your financial professional is aware of it, so that he or she knows it isn't necessary to build in an additional safety margin.

COMPLEMENTARY STAGES ON THE HOHO BUS TOUR

In thinking about mean reversion, one of the historical facts I use when thinking about my wife and myself is that growth-seeking assets have returned a positive average real return over periods of 5 consecutive years very roughly 75% of the time. This is shown in Stage I 21 in Route 2 (exploring investment), the stage that analyzes historical returns.

Thinking of risk tolerance (or risk aversion, the same thing in the opposite direction) generally, Stage H 62 in Route 1 (exploring happiness and the psychology of Life Two) goes into the fact that risk aversion tends to increase in Life Two, and Stage I 33 in Route 2 (exploring investment) sets out different ways of proceeding when partners have different attitudes towards risk.

Stages F 41 – F 46 in Route 4 (exploring retirement finance) go into detail on clear thinking about creating life income from your assets, and Stages F 51 – F 53 add a dose of reality to it all.

As mentioned more than once, Stage H 22 in Route 1 has the quote from my wise friend.

Take A Breath

I'm sure you don't realize what a profound exercise you've just been through.

My understanding is that few financial professionals check with you as to how your lifestyle is affected by changing asset values, and even fewer check how you'd feel about having to cut specific things out of your desired lifestyle.

In fact, this is a perspective that is often missing at a much more weighty level.

Think about all those massive pension funds you've heard about (and which you may even be a beneficiary of) – with millions or even billions of dollars. They have fiduciaries (trustees, whatever – the name varies from country to country) who are responsible for investing the assets and (in the case of "defined benefits" or "collective defined contribution" arrangements – the jargon isn't important) protecting the interests of the beneficiaries. How much risk do they feel comfortable taking, on your behalf?

Typically they go through a projection exercise, rather like using the PFR calculator, every few years to decide. But what *about trying to anticipate what they'd do if the assets suddenly fell by 10%, or 20%, or perhaps even more, as assets actually did in the global financial crisis of 2008-9? A professional in that field tells me that it's rare for them to think along those lines. If you were to ask the fiduciaries how they'd react, they could indeed think about it and respond – just as you did, in the last exercise. But it's not routine. That's the surprising thing. It's actually called "crisis management," and isn't typically done.*

You'd think that thinking about it before it actually happens, while you're still in good shape, rather than in the heat of a panicked reaction, would be routine with that magnitude of assets. But my professional friend experienced committees who kept thinking, "Let's not do anything yet, let's wait and see," while the situation worsened – they froze into inaction – whereas if they had been through the anticipatory exercise, they would clearly have decided to reduce their risk ("take risk off the table," as the jargon goes) and wouldn't have seen the situation sink as it did.

There's no question that thinking about the possibility in advance strengthens your resilience. If bad stuff happens to growth-seeking assets (as it inevitably does, periodically), it helps a lot to feel, "Well, I thought about the possibility when I was clear-headed, and so I won't panic now."

That's you. You've done a profound exercise. Congratulations.

***

OK, now let's put all our learning together in a financial plan.

Be aware that, in this plan, I'm focused purely on your lifestyle in Life Two. I'm not focused at all on your desire to buy a home, or insurance (though you could check out Stage F 13 in Route 4 on the Hoho Bus Tour, if those aspects are important for you). I'm not focused at all on any bequests that you may wish to leave, even though for most of us that's a very important set of considerations. (Check out Stage F 24 in Route 4 on the Hoho Bus Tour if that's relevant for you.) For all of that, consult with your family and your financial professional.

Those aspects go beyond the Walking Tour, though they're covered in the Hoho Bus Tour in the Stages I mentioned.

***

If you've already made the transition to Life Two, skip to Walk 21, because Walk 20 is for those who are still accumulating assets in Life One.

ACCUMULATING MONEY AND DRAWING IT DOWN GRADUALLY

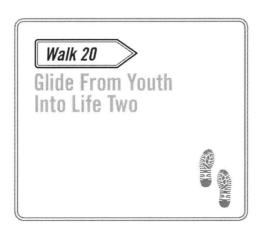

This is for those who are still accumulating assets, and haven't yet transitioned into Life Two. Through the story of how the global financial crisis and market crash of 2008 affected different members of a family in different ways, this Walk draws lessons for how the goals of growth and safety typically change as we age.

THE LEARNING

Americans introduced a simple but powerful concept for all of us who invest for retirement. They called it a glide path. It concerns your exposure to equities. Like a plane, your exposure should start high and glide gradually down over time as you approach retirement. How high it should start, and how low it should get at retirement: those are aspects that can and should be customized to your goals, your other sources of retirement income (such as the Pillar 1 pension) and your risk tolerance. But the notion of gliding down as you age is common to all such paths.

I could explain the rationale the way economists do, by referring to financial capital and human capital. But it's much more compelling to tell a story.

***

Once upon a time there was a family living in America. Dad was an investment geek, and the family endured his stories and lessons over the dinner table. He was fond of waving his arms and proclaiming that young people could invest 100% in equities without worrying. And the family was fond of Dad, tolerated him with affection, and generally ignored his well-meaning advice, whether on investment or anything else.

Son grew up, left home, got a job, and started investing in his company's retirement plan, called a 401(k) plan. He chose a fund that invested 100% in global equities. (He had remembered about global diversification.)

Along came the global financial crisis, and early in 2009 Son took his annual statement to Dad and, with a reproachful look, showed it to him.

Dad was ashamed that his first instinct was a feeling of pleasure that Son had actually listened to him about something. This was not par for the course. But he suppressed that feeling, since Son's look didn't just imply "Look what's happened to my assets." It was worse than that. It was more like "Look what you've done to me." Son was upset at the big loss, and at the very least needed empathy.

So Dad also suppressed the geeky responses that came to mind. He didn't say: "Did I ever tell you about mean reversion?" This is the notion that, over time, returns tend to revert to some sort of long-term average, and don't stay extreme for long. No, Son's money had depreciated permanently. Suggesting that the market would restore the loss wasn't credible.

He also didn't say: "Gosh, your fund only lost 30%. The global equity index lost 40%. You did 10% better than the index. People would kill for that sort of outperformance!" As another saying goes, you can't eat relative performance; losing less than others is no consolation.

So Dad said, "Yes, we've all lost money. This has been the worst market in two generations. The loss is beyond anything we ever seriously considered. The thing is, let's see how much of an impact it has on your goal, which is income security in retirement."

And Dad did a couple of rough calculations about how much income Son could reasonably expect at retirement at age 70. (After those dinner conversations, Son knew he wasn't likely to be able to retire earlier than 70. But that would still probably give him a generation of active enjoyment.) First Dad projected the income that might have accrued if the index hadn't gone down at all. Then he reduced the current assets by 30% and repeated the projection. And lo and behold, the projected income only decreased by 3%. Just a nuisance, rather than a tragedy.

How was that? No, not sleight of hand. The explanation was that 90% of the projected 401(k) income was due to come from Son's future savings. (Son was about 30 at the time, and hadn't been saving long.) That portion didn't suffer the market decline because it had not yet been saved. Only 10% of the projected retirement income was affected; a 30% loss there meant a 3% loss overall.

(For the geeks among you ... Economists would say that Son's retirement assets consisted, at that point, of 10% financial capital, invested in equities, and 90% in human capital – essentially future earning and saving power – and therefore not yet exposed to the market. If you assume that Son, through his accumulation years, has very roughly a "constant relative risk aversion," meaning a roughly constant tolerance for losing a proportion of aggregate retirement assets, then Son's aggregate retirement assets should have a roughly constant mix of growthy and safety-oriented assets. And if you consider human capital as broadly similar to index-linked safe investments rather than being growthy, then to achieve a constant aggregate exposure to growthy assets, Son's financial capital should have a gradually falling exposure to growthy assets as Son ages. See? Isn't this easier to understand via the story?)

Son absorbed this new perspective, this new framing of the issue, and was reassured by it. Then he asked: "How about you and Mom?" "Well," said Dad, "our retirement assets were only 50% in equities. But it has cost us 9% of our projected income."

In other words, even though Mom and Dad had only half of Son's equity exposure (50% compared with Son's 100%), they had actually taken three times as much risk. Why? Because the parents had much more in financial assets, and little human capital left.

**

And essentially that's the rationale for a glide path. Most of us must necessarily take some long-term risk (in the expectation of long-term reward) in order to achieve our retirement income goals, because the amount we need to save, if we focused just on risk-free assets, is typically beyond us. The glide path approach tells us something very important: that we shouldn't spread that long-term risk equally over our working lifetime. Instead, we should take much more at the start, when our financial capital is low, and reduce it as our financial capital increases.

Destination

When should we take investment risk? Mostly when we're young and have little financial capital at stake, less so when we mature and have much more financial capital at stake. So the shape of our risk-taking during our years of saving should follow a sort of glide path, from higher risk to lower risk.

EXERCISE

Apply the principle to yourself.

Are you a member of a "defined contribution" arrangement?

If so, what's the investment approach you use – one you decided yourself, or a so-called "target date glide path"?

Do you know why the particular approach or path you're in has the asset allocations associated with it?

What's the goal?

What's the risk?

Are you comfortable with them?

Do you have any personal assets or attributes that make you different from others of your age and gender?

Are you invested in inexpensive so-called "passive" investments or are you (implicitly) paying someone to make sure you do better than others?

In other words: do you understand your investment path and its rationale and cost?

COMPLEMENTARY STAGES ON THE HOHO BUS TOUR

Stage F 01 in Route 4 (exploring retirement finance) goes into detail on the point that, if we focus just on safety-oriented assets, the future savings required to preserve our lifestyle are typically far beyond us.

If you want to go more deeply into the use of target date funds and customizing them to reflect your circumstances that differ from those of the average participant for whom the glide path was designed, see Stage F 12 in Route 4 on the Hoho Bus Tour.

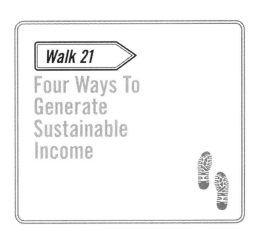

Walk 21

Four Ways To
Generate
Sustainable
Income

WHERE THE ROUTE TAKES US

So here we are, we've saved and invested, and we're ready to stop working and convert our assets from a lump sum into a flow of Life Two income that can be sustained for the rest of our lives. How can we do that? In this Walk we'll look at four approaches to making systematic withdrawals. They're none of them perfect; they all have pros and cons. Typically the approach used is one decided by your financial professional, but at the very least you should be aware of the pros and cons of each of them so that you can give your informed consent.

The learning

It's time to reach the climax of the Walking Tour. It's time to consider different ways of converting your accumulated assets into a lifetime income.

We remember that the big choice is between safety (enabling you to sleep well at night) and hoped-for but uncertain asset growth (enabling you to eat well, but compromising sleep). And we also remember that the biggest fear of retirees, according to surveys, is outliving their assets. Sleeping well is therefore the higher priority. And that in turn implies that the essential feature is that Life Two income must last a lifetime.

Of course, some retirees have enough that they can live their desired lifestyle and still not outlive their assets. Others have so little that the essentials of life are all they can afford. Neither of these groups, for entirely different reasons, is forced to choose between eating well and sleeping well. One group can sleep well, no matter what. The other group struggles to achieve either goal. It's the group in between that is faced with difficult choices, because they have to decide on where they are most comfortable (or perhaps least uncomfortable) as they consider the trade-off implicit in setting eating well against sleeping well.

In this Walk I'll outline four ways in which your accumulated assets can be made to generate income that's reasonably sustainable over your lifetime.

As an overview, these are the four ways:

1. Buy an immediate lifetime income annuity.
2. Draw down an amount each year that is based on your future longevity at the start of each year.
3. Buy longevity insurance (also called an advanced life deferred annuity), and draw down an amount each year from your remaining assets that is designed to last until your longevity insurance kicks in.
4. Assume death at some advanced age, and draw down

an amount each year that is designed to last until that advanced age.

***

Buying an immediate lifetime income annuity used to be the only way permitted in the UK until 2015. Its advantages are that the income lasts for life, regardless of how long that may be, and that there is no cheaper way to guarantee any level of income for life.

Why then do most people shun it (except, as it happens, in Chile)?

One reason is that people instinctively compare the lump sum with the annual income. Dr Meir Statman eloquently recounts the regret of an annuity-purchasing friend, quoting him as saying, "Yesterday I was a millionaire. Today I'm living on $79,700 a year" – and that was in the good old days of high interest rates.

A second reason is loss of control. The lump sum is gone and the deal is irreversible. Your portfolio flexibility has gone with it.

A third reason is that in effect a lifetime income annuity is effectively a fixed income investment: pure safety. The ability to take some growth risk vanishes.

And a fourth reason is that it may feel like a gamble: early death causes a huge loss. (In fact, conceptually longevity insurance is typically a more sensible option, though it isn't widely available outside the USA. See the complementary stages for more on this.)

So, as with most financial issues, there are trade-offs to be considered and the cheapest and most certain way of creating income for life will appeal to some and not to others.

***

In the second approach, each year's drawdown is based on your future longevity. This is a straightforward concept.

Suppose you have $200,000 in accumulated assets, and your future longevity is 16.2 years. Divide the $200,000 by 16.2, and you get $12,346. That's how much you draw down in the coming year.

The concept is simple. If you live exactly as long as your future expectancy, and earn no investment return, the annual $12,346 will last exactly the right length of time. Problem solved.

In fact you can invest the money any way you like, with whatever combination of safety and growth you feel comfortable with. Since your drawdown left some balance ($187,654, if you withdrew the amount on the first day of the year), there will be some asset value (the balance adjusted by the investment return) remaining at the end of the year. Let's say the new balance is $190,000.

At the start of the next year you are one year older. You still have a future life expectancy, though it's a now little bit shorter than 16.2 years. Let say it's 15.5 years. OK, divide the $190,000 by 15.5, and withdraw $12,258. And so on.

There is always some balance in your assets. They never decline to zero. There is always some future life expectancy as long as you're alive. And so the process continues. (It's a standard approach in the USA, called a "required minimum distribution.")

The advantages of this approach are that it guarantees some income for life, and it permits whatever asset allocation you are comfortable with.

The main disadvantage is that the amount of income is both variable and uncertain, because there is no certainty to the future investment return that your assets will earn.

A second disadvantage is that over time, as future life expectancy decreases, the proportion of the assets withdrawn each year becomes large, depleting them faster and resulting in drawdowns that become much smaller later in life. A partial solution to this problem is to add some number each year (like 6 years) to the future life expectancy, and then apply this approach. Of course the drawdowns are smaller, but the decline later is not nearly as rapid.

***

With the third approach (which I explain here for completeness, even though it isn't available in many countries), you pay a lump sum to purchase longevity insurance, which is an income for the balance of your life, commencing on some future date (the deferred date) if you are still alive then. For example: you're 65 and pay a lump sum that guarantees that, if you reach age 85, from then onward you'll get an income for as long as you live.

The rest of your assets then only have to last until that deferred date. The financial impact of your longevity uncertainty has gone, and you have the simpler task of drawing down some regular amount from your assets until the deferred date.

The main benefit of this approach is that you pay relatively little for longevity protection, while preserving the control, the flexibility and the liquidity of maintaining the rest of your assets for drawdowns.

A disadvantage relative to buying an immediate annuity is that you implicitly pay more for your longevity protection.

Also, as with any approach where you maintain control of your assets, your drawdown will be variable and will depend on the extent to which you seek growth for your assets, since growth is inevitably uncertain and variable.

***

In the fourth approach you essentially self-insure your longevity risk, by choosing some advanced age (like 95 or 100) and arranging your drawdowns to last until the end of that distant horizon. This is the approach for which the longevity stuff in Walk 13 is directly relevant.

This approach has the benefit of preserving control, flexibility and liquidity in your assets. The main disadvantage is that it's the most expensive way to deal with longevity uncertainty, since you don't pool your longevity risk with that of others, and pooling is the way to reduce or minimize the cost of longevity protection. It's like arranging to have sufficient assets to replace your home and its contents in the event of a fire, rather than paying an insurance premium.

***

I've set out the pros and cons of each approach so that you can decide which of them suits you best psychologically, before you find a professional to do the actual drawdown calculation. (I'm guessing that most of you won't do it yourself.)

Of course you may find that you're unable to decide conclusively between, let's say, two of these ways. Or that you prefer one and your partner prefers another – because there's no reason why partners should have identical mindsets, even though risk profile questionnaires typically gloss over this difference. In which case you could use both ways, dividing your assets between them.

DESTINATION

There are four ways to generate retirement income from your accumulated assets: buy an immediate lifetime income annuity; draw down an amount each year that depends on your future life expectancy; buy longevity insurance and use the fixed period until it kicks in as the period over which you calculate a sustainable drawdown; calculate a sustainable drawdown until some fixed advanced age.

It's important for you to choose between them because they have very different characteristics.

EXERCISE

If you want to understand the pros and cons in greater detail, and your professional appears to want to use one approach without consideration of the others, you may want to look at Stages F 62 – F 65 on the Hoho Bus Tour.

Regardless, here are some aspects you may want to be clear about, in giving your informed consent:

Does your professional appear to want to use one approach without consideration of the others?

Do you understand how your periodic withdrawals will be calculated and arranged?

Are you comfortable, in particular, with the possible cons of the arrangement?

Is your approach one that can be changed later, if circumstances suggest it, or are you locked in once you start or have to pay a large penalty to change?

Do you understand whether the probable stream of withdrawals will increase or decrease over time?

Do you understand what happens on the passing of either you or your partner?

COMPLEMENTARY STAGES ON THE HOHO BUS TOUR

Stage F 28 in Route 4 (exploring retirement finance) shows how people with different Personal Funded Ratios face different types of financial choices.

The four ways of generating sustainable income in Life Two are discussed in greater detail in Stages F 62 – F 65 in Route 4. In addition, Stage F 71 shows a case study.

The fact that there is no cheaper way to sustain income throughout Life Two than via an immediate lifetime income annuity, and other characteristics of immediate annuities, are explained in detail in Stages T 05 – T 08 in the Trail for Enthusiasts.

See Stage L 31 in Route 3 (exploring longevity) and Stage T 09 in the Trail for Enthusiasts for the distinction between longevity insurance and an immediate lifetime income annuity.

Stage F 72 shows the choices available if your home is part of the portfolio that is needed to generate your Life Two income.

Take A Breath

Whether or not you realize it, we're pretty much done, as far as the three sets of issues that we started with are concerned.

Remember them? "Will I lose my identity?" "How will I spend my time?" "Will I outlive my assets?" That was a long time ago, wasn't it! Now you've answered all three questions. And I hope you feel much better grounded, with your fears about Life Two replaced by knowledge of where you stand.

***

I thought it might be useful to end the Walking Tour with two final angles. One brings together the elements of your first conversation with your financial professional. The other considers how you might keep your loved ones informed about your plans.

In effect, you are now bringing guests into the land of Life Two, where you yourself are comfortable. That's quite a transformation from the time before you started this Walking Tour. My congratulations to you!

YOU'RE DONE! WELCOME YOUR GUESTS TO LIFE TWO

Walk 22

Your First
Conversation
With A Financial
Professional

WHERE THE ROUTE TAKES US

If you do search for and find a financial professional, what sorts of skills are relevant? What kinds of attitudes might you seek in the relationship? What might you talk about? We'll look at those questions in this Walk.

The learning

All the way through I've deliberately referred to your "financial professional," even though in different countries people in the financial industry have different titles and affiliations. I have two reasons for doing this. One is that I don't want to be tied to a term used in only one country, because then readers in other countries won't recognize whom I'm talking about. The other is that, in searching for a generic word I could use, I find "professional" particularly appealing. It's generic, of course. But in addition it has a particular connotation, implying not only competence but also behaving with the client's interests at heart – as a professional, rather than just as a member of the financial industry.

How might you find one? Often people simply use their bank. Or you might seek references from people you trust. Or look at advertisements. The approach may be different in different countries, depending on how easy it is to find professionals in your field of search.

You might also have different fields of search. For example: planning your income for Life Two, investments, taxation, insurance, estate planning, long-term care – there's no end to the things you might seek expertise about. And you might use one professional for all your needs, or several members in the same firm or partnership, or several individuals or firms or partnerships – in which case some co-ordination might be useful to ensure that all the relevant bases are covered and dealt with in a consistent way.

In this Walk I'll outline the kinds of things you and your professional might talk about.

***

One important aspect is to understand whether or not your professional is prepared to act as a fiduciary – regardless of whether or not fiduciary duty is required by law. This is an issue that is relevant around the world, and different countries have dealt with it in different ways, and have different (or no) degrees of compulsion for professionals to act as fiduciaries. So let's spend a little time on it.

What's a fiduciary? Simply, a fiduciary is someone who represents you in a trusted capacity, acting in an ethical way in your best interests.

Doesn't everybody behave this way? Not necessarily. Many professionals have conflicts of interest.

What's a conflict of interest? Here's a definition taken from the 'Lectric Law Library on the internet.[26]

CONFLICT OF INTEREST – Refers to a situation when someone, such as a lawyer or public official, has competing professional or personal obligations or personal or financial interests that would make it difficult to fulfill his duties fairly.

What should you do if you discover such a situation? Here are some thoughts.

Are conflicts common? Yes. They are the stuff of life. The world is a complex place. We all have incentives, some direct and some indirect, some financial and some emotional, that influence us. Conflicts are not a one-size-fits-all situation. Some conflicts are serious, some are minor.

With professionals, the source of a conflict is typically that they know a lot more than you do about their field of expertise. You want them to use that information to do the best for you. Their proposed solution may benefit them as well as benefiting you. Which is the dominant motivation, their own benefit or yours? If it's clearly for your best interest, that's fine. If it's for theirs, that may still be acceptable, if their interest coincides with yours, or it may not be, if their interest acts against yours. Sometimes it's difficult to judge.

But the point is that you should at least be aware of it, and it should be your judgment to make (not the professional's) as to whether, in the circumstances, it's a big deal or virtually irrelevant. And so the simplest, most direct starting point is to ask your prospective professional if he or she is acting, or will act, in a fiduciary capacity, and to get the response in writing. That's because the alternative to a fiduciary relationship is "buyer beware," meaning you're on your own as far as your interests are concerned.

Note that this doesn't mean that the end objective is total avoidance of conflicts: in their commercial guise they may be unavoidable. The operative principle here is "trust, but verify" – the Russian phrase that Reagan said he and Gorbachev should use as an operating principle as they undertook nuclear disarmament. (In the original Russian it rhymes: "doveryai, no proveryai," making the phrase memorable in Russian but not in English.)

**

Another important aspect is for both you and your professional to understand and agree to the nature of your relationship. In this regard I'm grateful for the unique insights of Bill Horton, developed when he worked as the Chief Investment Officer for MD Financial, a firm offering financial advice and investment services to Canadian physicians. He observed that doctors play many different roles with their patients, and when doctors become, in effect, financial patients, they demand the same variety of roles in their relationship with the professionals who are, in effect, their financial doctors.

Specifically, a professional's role can be paternalistic (acting as a sort of guardian), informative (where the professional is the competent technical expert), interpretive (acting as counselor or adviser), or deliberative (acting as friend or teacher). Of course these roles exist on a continuum; they blend into one another, rather than being separate; and the relationship can encompass more than one role, and can change over time.

The appropriate role, observes Bill, is highly dependent on the patient's (that is, your) beliefs, knowledge and desired level of autonomy. So, go back to Walk 3 and review what it means to be an informed consumer of expertise, and then decide what sort of role you'd like your professional to play in your relationship. And explain this to your professional, so that you both have the same understanding of the relationship.

***

What else might you ask your professional before starting a relationship?

Well, consider what information you have to give a bank before the bank will agree to lend you money. Typically, you have to inform them about your financial position (income, assets, liabilities, that sort of thing – indeed, some history of these things), how you propose to use the money you're asking to borrow, what security you offer, what progress reports you need to submit, and so on. It makes sense that if you are going to entrust a bank with investing your assets, you will demand comparable information from the bank. Your assets represent hard-earned money; it is much more significant to you than the loan is to the bank. And the same holds for any professional to whom you are entrusting the management of all or part of your assets.

What might be comparable information? Well, being told "Trust me, I'm good and I have great references" doesn't even start to be enough! There isn't a definitive list of questions. But in general you need to find out about things like their credentials, the scope of their investment or advisory practice, and the profitability of the practice. What is their philosophy in dealing with people like you? Whom will you be dealing with? Who are the support staff you'll be dealing with?

By the way, don't be upset with being told you'll be dealing mostly with support staff. Think how much more efficient your doctor or dentist or lawyer can be, dealing with a much larger practice when much of the work is done by specialized staff members and you only see the professional briefly. If every visit were to be a one-on-one with the professional, there would be far fewer clients – and each client would have to pay much more.

Of course, in turn you'll tell the professional what are your hopes and fears. But in addition, tell the professional what you've learned from the Walking Tour. Different readers will get different things from it. That's fine. But your revelations will be a good start to a deeper discussion of how your learnings and your knowledge and your goals and feelings will mesh with the professional's philosophy and practice. And in turn that will help you decide if the professional seems to be a good fit with you.

***

One important point is that you shouldn't have to learn a new language. By this I mean that professionals shouldn't explain what they do for you in investment or any other technical terms. "Standard deviation," "downside protection," "risk-return trade-off," "normal distribution" (or worse, "skewed distribution") – that sort of stuff is fine when they're talking to one another. On their specialized technical island, that's their language. It's jargon, a sort of shorthand that they understand. But when they encounter someone from the mainland (you!), they need to translate their island lingo into mainland-speak, and talk to you in a way you understand. Many will tell you that this is exactly what they do. Well, one test is how clearly they ask questions in their risk questionnaire. Another is what their standard (monthly, quarterly, annual) reports to clients look like. Ask to see these, and judge for yourself.

***

There's one more very important aspect to be aware of and to discuss with your financial professional. And that's fees. Advice or any form of assistance with your Life Two financial planning can be very useful. And so you should expect to pay for it. The relevant questions are: how will you pay, and how much?

A problem is that sometimes services may *appear* to be free because you are not billed explicitly for it. (And many buyers of services – that is, people like you – prefer it that way. They prefer not to think about it or to have to write a check for it.) Clearly, when you seek advice or assistance the main thing you're looking for is the competence of the person or firm you hire. But among your search criteria should be that you get a clear understanding of how your professional (or, more generally, your professional's firm) will be paid. And since there are multiple ways of remuneration, and payments for multiple services may be bundled into a single amount or formula, you should be aware of the unbundled (that is, separate) amounts of remuneration for the different services. That's the only way you can compare the charges for the services you'll receive.

Payments to a professional's firm tend to be of two main types. One is an explicit fee that you pay directly, of a size independent of the amount of assets under consideration. The other is a commission (or equivalent) paid by an investment manager to your professional's firm, for directing your assets to that investment manager, typically explicitly tied to the amount of assets under consideration. (Sometimes your professional's firm is itself the investment manager.) Confusingly, sometimes remuneration is called fee-based, giving the impression that it's independent of asset size, when in fact it is based on asset size after all. And some forms of remuneration are a combination of fees and commission equivalents. So: buyer beware, and be aware.

The main forms of fee-only asset-independent remuneration that you might pay to a professional's firm are as follows:

- A one-time fee for a one-time service.
- A flat retainer fee (for example, so much a quarter or a year) for services that will be ongoing.
- An hourly fee for services that will be ongoing.

The main forms of asset-based (which I also refer to as commission-equivalent) remuneration paid by an investment institution or indirectly by you to a professional's firm are as follows:

- *A front-end load.* This is an amount paid at the start. Typically it means that the amount that will be invested for you is reduced by an amount related to the front-end load.
- *A back-end load.* This is an alternative to the front-end load. Under this arrangement the payment is made to the professional's firm at the start, and the full amount of your assets will be invested. But if you withdraw the investment

before some specified period of time, there may well be a form of surrender charge applied, to offset the up-front payment.

- *A trailer.* Under this arrangement the professional's firm is paid a (smaller) amount periodically (such as every month or quarter or year) as long as your investment stays in the fund into which it is initially placed.

As you will have guessed by now, some commission-type arrangements involve both a front-end or back-end load as well as a trailer.

Asset-based commission-type arrangements have been very popular with advisory firms. They're virtually invisible to you, if they're taken directly out of the fund. Obviously they have an impact by reducing what would otherwise be the value of your assets, but if all you see is an end-of-year value of assets, you won't see explicitly how much the value has been reduced because of the professional firm's compensation. And many buyers of services – that is, people like you – are perverse, in the sense that they will live happily with a concealed asset-based commission but be appalled by a much smaller explicit fee. This makes it much more convenient for a professional firm for remuneration to come from a commission; and since commissions vary from one kind of investment product to another, it is tempting to place your assets in a high-commission arrangement rather than a low-commission arrangement.

In some countries legislation has therefore been passed banning commission-type remuneration. And in some countries there is also legislation that binds the professional to give advice that is solely based on what's in your best interest (in other words, a fiduciary relationship, as discussed at the start of this Walk).

One other aspect is that your professional may place your investments in what are known as "actively managed" (as opposed to "passive index-tracking") funds. Whether your investments should be active or passive is a separate issue, and you might want to look at the complementary stages listed at the end of the Walk.

The connection with fees is that active investing is much more expensive than passive investing, for the investment management company offering the service. It is also typically more profitable, so the company pays higher commissions for active than for passive. The higher cost of active management may be in addition to the remuneration of your professional's firm. By the time your professional firm's own fees are added, the total charge to you may be noticeably high.

Where there is legislation requiring a fiduciary standard of conduct and explicit fees, commentators predict that buyers of services (that is, people like you) will be more inclined to ask for passive management in order to reduce aggregate visible fees, or that professionals will be more inclined to place you in passive investment products for the same reason.

Gosh, that's a lot to absorb, isn't it! But it's worth knowing about, because fees can be very high.

One quick but excellent way to get an initial idea of how much of any investment return over the long term you will keep, and how much you will sacrifice because of fees, is to use an online calculator called T-REX (for Total Return Efficiency Index)[27] developed by author Larry Bates in connection with his book *Beat the Bank*.[28]

In the standard example on the first page of this online calculator, in which the professional charges an annual fee of 1.75% of the assets under investment, those assets earning an annual return of 6.4%, over a 25-year period the proportion of the overall investment return actually credited to the owner of the assets is 57% of the total return. Yes, in that example almost half of the return is eaten up in relatively opaque fees.

Your situation may be better or worse. That's not my point. My point is that you should be aware of it, because yes, it really can be that important.

DESTINATION

Interview prospective financial professionals to find out not only relevant information about their practice, but also their philosophy, how they propose to interact with you, whether they are prepared to act as a fiduciary, whether they communicate in their language or yours, and what fees you will be charged.

Exercise

Prepare a list of things you want to know about your prospective financial professional.

Prepare a list of things he or she needs to know about that most important person: you! Not just your financial situation and goals, but your hopes and fears, from Walk 3. Remember your objective is to feel that there's a good fit between you and your professional, and that it's solely your interests that are relevant.

Calculate your T-REX score, if you already have investments administered by a financial professional.

Complementary stages on the Hoho Bus Tour

Stages I 41 – I 44 in Route 2 (exploring investment) go into some detail about active and passive management of assets.

Walk 23

Talking To Your
Adult Children
About This Phase
Of Life

WHERE THE ROUTE TAKES US

Now that things are in order for you, you might want to ensure that they're also in order if anything happens to you. There are many reasons why parents are uncomfortable to talk to their adult children about personal matters. This Walk identifies some of the benefits of that kind of conversation.

The learning

This Walk deals with talking to your adult children (or, of course, other close family members) about your investments and more generally about your goals and plans. I first did this some years ago, when I decided to graduate from full-time work. Most retirees find, after time passes, that it's useful to repeat the exercise, as circumstances change and nothing ever works out quite how you projected. It then could become the year's most important focal point. (Memo to myself…)

I realize that some families (particularly in generations past) have found it very difficult to discuss any aspect at all of this phase of life with their adult children. Neither my wife Susan nor I ever had such a conversation with our parents.

***

Our first effort with our own children has gone down in family history as Dad's Decumulation Talk. Yes, as you might guess, I did most of the talking. Just before we started Susan, without saying a word, placed a cartoon in front of me.[29] (It has become a family favorite.)

I got permission from the New Yorker to reproduce the cartoon here.

*"Before we begin this family meeting, how about we go around
and say our names and a little something about ourselves."*

I got the message: "Remember you're their father, not a businessman." I'm told I conducted myself appropriately. It turned out that this became a real bonding experience in the family, and one of the consequences is that we've been able to discuss financial matters with our children, not only our matters but also theirs, ever since – they've asked for our input from time to time, with issues on which they thought we could help.

At the time I gave them a document entitled "Goals and Plans," which we prepared in order to give them enough background that, if and when the need arose, they could be confident about making decisions for us. I'm including an outline of what our document contained as an appendix at the end of this Walk, in the hope that it might be of help to you. A number of clients asked for it when I mentioned it in a talk a few months after I graduated from full-time work.

Since then I've done some research and discovered a lot of useful information. I'll set out some of it here; but of course you'll understand that this is simply meant as educational background, not to be a comprehensive list, and that there's no substitute for talking to your legal and financial professionals. And also that, when I refer to your adult children, that's a generic way of saying "whoever it is that you'd like to have take charge of your affairs, during or after your lifetime" – and that might perhaps be a professional or a financial institution, not just a family member.

**

I've found it helpful to think of three dimensions regarding the information to be shared.

The first dimension is a list of important documents and where they are to be found (preferably in one place, known to your children). This includes government-issued documents relating to your identity (birth, marriage, citizenship, whatever).

Also include information regarding assets and liabilities, such as home ownership, cars, bank accounts, savings bonds, credit cards, life insurance, savings plans related to work or retirement, other invested assets, other miscellaneous things you own – that sort of thing.

Of course there are also important legal documents under this heading, such as your will, a power of attorney, and advance directives, like a living will, medical power of attorney, end-of-life instructions, and so on. (There are many flavors of these and they have different names in different countries.) And people they should contact, and their contact details: not just professionals like your doctor, your lawyer, your financial professional, but also close friends and relatives.

One side issue, relating to wills. It's often said that many people die without a will. My father-in-law, who was in the insurance business, taught me that everybody already has a will. A will is a document that says what will happen to your estate after you're gone. In many countries the law says what will happen, if you haven't written your own document. So think of the law as your will. You do have a will, no matter what you think – it just may be that somebody else wrote it for you. Better to override it with your own wishes!

The second dimension relates to levels of involvement.[30] The least involved level is where your children know where to find the information mentioned earlier.

Next, you may want to share some of the actual information with them, such as your finances and your will. (As you can see from my anecdote at the start, Susan and I decided to start here.) Once you start doing this, you will probably want to repeat the exercise periodically, as we now plan to do.

At this stage you're still in full control. It may later become necessary for them to assist you, or to share responsibility for your affairs, or to take over that responsibility completely.

A friend who was going through her own parents' late phase of life reminded me that, in that phase, the relationship between parents and children can change completely. The parents need the children, rather than the other way around. The parents can become fragile and susceptible, and easy to be taken advantage of. The children worry about the parents, and have to soothe them. My friend added, feelingly: "I don't know what I'd do if I couldn't trust someone to take care of me ..."

No doubt, therefore, you will have consulted your children before making the required arrangements, and got their agreement to whatever goes into the relevant documents. And you'll have given them a list of the medications you take, and ensured that your professionals know they should consult your children and also know where to find them.

It can provide great peace of mind to know that all of this has been discussed before the need for the arrangements to be carried out ever arises – even if one day you may not remember ever having done this.

It's peace of mind not only for you but also for your children, who may be worried about whether they'll have to support you financially at the end. For your children's sake, don't leave this conversation so late that your mental capacity is declining and you still haven't had the conversation.

And that leads to *the third dimension*, which involves saving trouble for your executor after your "estate event." (You'll recall from Walk 13 that some American insurance agents don't like talking about death.)

Some wills are hotly contested by family members who can't stand one another. If that's the family attitude, you may not be able to solve this problem while you're alive.

The angst that it may be possible for you to spare your executor arises from the small things, like dividing up your personal possessions, when different family members each want the same thing, or think that a particular apportionment or process of deciding is unfair.

I refer you to an article I particularly liked on the subject, by Paul Sullivan in The New York Times.[31] A quote from the piece: "... just think for a second what it would be like on Christmas morning if your children ran downstairs and there were all of these presents, bright and shining, big and small, but with no name tags on them. Can you imagine the free-for-all that would ensue?"

That got to me, and that's why I include it here, even though it probably won't make any list of really important financial things to consider. But emotional things? Yes indeed! And those are important too.

***

This piece triggered emotional reader reaction when I posted a version of it on my website.

One wrote a moving (and yet funny) account of his family dialogue, after he initially did things himself and then thought to tell them what would happen after he passed.

Another wrote that this particular post hit him hard, like with a 2x4. He added: "This is the jolt I have needed and my 2018 goal is not only to read the blogs, but also to actively plan and execute, based on them, as applicable to my needs. Thank you Don."

It's gratifying when a blog post creates a teachable moment for a reader.

DESTINATION

Share information with your adult children: about your current finances, about your desires if you should become incapacitated, and about your will.

APPENDIX: OUTLINE OF THE FIRST EZRA "GOALS AND PLANS" DOCUMENT

1. Introduction: Purpose, summary, appreciation of good fortune, request for intervention if and when required

2. Goals
   • For ourselves: continuation of lifestyle
   • For our beneficiaries: during our lives, and after our second estate event

3. Background
   • What we've done, financially, over the years, and why

4. Our assets and liabilities, their current values and details of where they are located

5. Our lifestyle and other outflows
   • The normal budget for our spending and saving
   • Exceptional planned expenditures
   • Life insurance, long term care, other partial hedges against the vicissitudes of life

6. Lifestyle versus assets
   • Latest "personal funded ratio" calculations
   • Dials to be turned: why, and how much
   • Caution: transition means this isn't carved in stone
   • Contact details for our financial professional

7. Current and future plans: what, when and how long
   • Work
   • Lifestyle

- Real estate: downsize, move, perhaps rent, perhaps one day a reverse mortgage
- Reassess every year, with a big review at age 70
- When to start taking Social Security, and why
- Rearrange the assets at age 70
- Where there are still elements of flexibility
- Reminder of the life abundance portfolio as a framework: family and friends, work and play, mental and physical health, finances

Exercise

There's a long implicit to-do list in the Walk. Go through it systematically. If not now, when?

Take your time over it.

There may well be aspects of your situation that I don't cover in the stage. If you feel able to do it, ask your loved ones for their suggestions too.

Once you've done this, you'll all feel much more comfortable – and, I'm sure, even closer to one another. So repeat it periodically.

Complementary stages on the Hoho Bus Tour

Stage F 52 in Route 4 (exploring retirement finance) mentions three things that can derail your plan: long life, illness and cognitive decline.

WHERE THE ROUTE TAKES US

Take time out to celebrate! I hope you feel proud of yourself and much further along than you ever thought you'd be. I hope you now feel in control. After all, you've explored the territory, you understand the basic framework, and you have actually applied it to yourself. You have a plan, and if you seek expertise, you know how to make the most of it, and how to help the experts apply their expertise to your own specific situation.

My congratulations to you

Congratulations! You may not realize what an elite group you now belong to.

But first, allow me to remind you about some of the things you now know and what they enable you to do.

You know that graduating from full-time work is not necessarily a straightforward thing, that it usually requires a psychological shift, but that it's a change that also creates an opportunity to redefine yourself, and to re-organize how you spend your time in a way that makes you happy. And you've also seen the benefits of talking to your adult children about the future as you'd like it to be.

You now understand the concept of longevity. For most, the odds are that your future life expectancy is longer than you thought.

You know that there are only two investments goals, safety and growth. There's no "right" mixture of the two for you; what's appropriate depends partly on your financial circumstances and partly on whether you can sleep well while you hope for the growth that will enable you to eat as well as you desire.

The way your asset portfolio is structured will now reflect your risk tolerance, which has been personalized by considering how you would feel if you couldn't live your desired lifestyle to the fullest extent.

And you know there are four ways to convert assets into a stream of income that will be sustainable throughout Life Two.

Wow! How much of all that did you know before you started?

If you were an average person before you started (and you're certainly not one now, you're far, far above that level), you probably knew almost none of that.

What does that now mean to you?

For most people, planning for Life Two is a mysterious, confusing subject that's best avoided because it causes anxiety and the only way to escape that anxiety is to avoid thinking about it. Not for you, any more. Now you have a framework in which to consider issues, and a starting perspective on them. Now the thought process is manageable. In fact, now you're in control. The mystery is gone. That's powerfully reassuring and energizing.

Now you're in a position to help experts to help you. Even better, as a genuinely informed consumer of their expertise, you can assess their advice, challenge their findings, and consider whether their recommendations fit your own situation. That's a subject – your own situation, your own goals and attitudes – that you know better than the experts, and now you can move forward with confidence. Not with certainty, because nobody has a crystal ball, but with far greater confidence than the average person. I wish I could offer you a crystal ball too, but ... yes, I imagine you're smiling.

Let me help you to feel superior!

I've worked in this field from the earliest days of "defined contribution" or "accumulation" pensions. For convenience, professionals divide participants into three groups, for investment purposes, according to the participants' attitude: "do it for me" (those who are content to elect a default investment option, like a target date fund), "do it with me" (those who make some personal choices away from purely following the default option), and "do it myself" (those who want complete control over all the investment decisions in their personal account). Yes, if you remember the box in Walk 2, it was a variation of my own learning from my professional career.

Guess what? The vast majority are in the "do it for me" category. Sometimes as many as 90% of participants in a plan elect the default option, for participation, for the amount they save or for their investment path. Of course, it's possible that some of these participants have thought things through and concluded that the default is just right for them. My experience tells me that would be rare. Typically it's just because it saves thinking, it saves confusion.

And now you've consciously risen above that. What's more, even among the "do it with me" group there tend to be very few who think beyond investing, who think, in addition, about psychology, longevity and finance. So you can just imagine what a tiny percentage know anything like as much as you now do.

And that's why I congratulate you. You've made huge progress. Well done!

Perhaps that's as far as you want to go. That's fine. By completing the Walking Tour, you've made huge progress. That's why I congratulate you. Again, well done!

You may be feeling pumped up now, wanting to take your inquisitiveness on some topics further. In which case, I simply say "au revoir," which means "until we meet again." That's what the Hoho Bus Tour is for. I await your pleasure.

I wish I could go further. That's how much fun it has been for me, designing and conducting this Walking Tour. But you're a busy person, and I won't take up any more of your time. Thank you for your company!

Exercise

Your celebration – in whatever form you decide!

Toast yourself – you've earned it. You've gone way further than most people.

Congratulations!

ENDNOTES

1 Jacobson (2011).

2 Aaker et al (2011).

3 Gilbert (2006).

4 Dunn et al (2011).

5 Crosby (2017).

6 Levinson (1976).

7 Carstensen (2011).

8 Covey (1989).

9 http://www.boominglives.co.uk/week-1-the-transition-from-work-posted-11th-november-2016/

10 Kinder (2000).

11 Zelinski (2009).

12 Claxton (1997).

13 Tony Parsons, if you ever see this, my eternal thanks for your wisdom.

14 Melone (2016).

15 See, for example, Ashford (2016), Hogan (2013), Kalish (2011).

16 Smith et al (2016).

17 Bernstein (2014).

18 Clements (2018).

19 http://www.gallup.com/poll/162872/one-three-americans-prepare-detailed-household-budget.aspx

20 MacDonald et al (2016).

21 Hamilton (2015) and Vettese (2015).

22 As at March 17, 2018.

23 Also as at March 17, 2018.

24 World Bank (1994).

25 Flemming vs Nestor, 1960.

26 www.lectlaw.com.

27 http://larrybates.ca/t-rex-score/

28 Bates (2018).

29 It's by Matthew Diffee, published in *New Yorker*, January 28, 2002.

30 I found this angle in Anderson Elder Law (2015).

31 Sullivan (2016).

THANKS

As this list grew, so did my gratitude. I'm very lucky. I just have a nagging feeling that, despite its length, I've forgotten some names. In which case, let me know, and please accept my apologies.

This first group of friends told me how they're thinking about retirement, and their honesty was the start of my journey. Thanks very much to Fatima Ali, Patricia Chiavuzzo, Kathleen and Ron Clark, James Fraser, Brian Goguen, Adam Hornung, Jacqueline Jamieson, Saima Khan, Renata Klemensowicz, Shailesh Kshatriya, Tom Lappalainen, Mary Beth Lato, Jack Lin, Yoshi Maeda, Maria Nastasi, Kate Nowak and Jason Self. A special double thanks to Renata and Yoshi, who contributed specific content as well.

For more general discussions over extended periods of time, my thanks to Irshaad Ahmad, Mike Clark, Bruce Curwood, Randy Gunn, Graham Harman, John Horwood, Kendra Kaake, David Knox, Tim Noonan, Keith Pangretitsch, Bob Schmidt, Nick Spencer and Ian Toner.

And taking that even further, lifetimes of wisdom contributed to my education, from Keith Ambachtsheer, Laura Carstensen, Bob Collie, Barry Gillman, Russ Hill, Theo Kocken, Moshe Milevsky, Arun Muralidhar, Wade Pfau, Bill Sharpe, Meir Statman and Geoff Warren. They helped shape me. For better or for worse, my gratitude and thanks! (I follow Wade's website https://retirementresearcher.com.)

For comments on the manuscript at various stages, my thanks to Xerxes Bamji, Chantal Bray, Roger Breeden, Sally Bridgeland, Simon Chinnery, Michael Clancy, Bob Collie, Jens van Egmond, Bill Falloon, Cedric Fan, Tim Furlan, Mike Hannon, Ted Harris,

David Hartley, Ralph Loader, Rosemary Meier, Thomas Philips, Cheryl Swanberg and J J Woolverton.

With some I included specific ideas that they brought to my mind, so special thanks to Janine Baldridge, Larry Bates, Michelle Cracknell, Ralph Frank, John Gillies, Bill Horton, Peter Kolthof, Alex Mazer and Michael Thomas.

An enormous amount of very practical hands-on corporate experience was willingly provided to me by Cindy Deere, Reg Hinkley, Chris Hogg, Jasbir Holait, Martin Mannion and Dame Jane Newell. Abundant thanks to them.

To Claer Barrett and her award-winning team at *FT Money*, including Josephine Cumbo and James Pickford, my thanks for their encouragement and willingness to give me an occasional column called The Art of Investment, and for permission to use material that was first published there.

Many others also helped me reach a broader public, and my gratitude goes to them. Graham Hand at Cuffelinks, Bill Robson at the C D Howe Institute, Joanne Segars at what used to be the UK's National Association of Pension Funds (now the Pensions and Lifetime Savings Association), the team at *Pensions & Investments* (Chris Battaglia, Nikki Pirrello, Amy Resnick), the team at the World Pension Summit (Eric Eggink, Harry Smorenberg, Mirjam Guldemond), Jason Parker at Sound Retirement Planning, Bryan Weeks at Russell Investments – my thanks for their immense help.

My thanks for a decade of intellectual stimulation to the Avida team: Stan Beckers, Paul Boerboom, Sally Bridgeland, Gordon Clark, Dorothee Franzen, Bart Heenk, Peter Kolthof.

Nico Aspinall, Jonathan Clements, David Feather, David Knox, Richard Owen, Dallas Salisbury, Idan Shlesinger, Kevin Turner and Ernie Zelinski: in different ways, each has encouraged me, and I thank them for their contributions, even if they weren't aware of it! (I follow Jonathan's website https://humbledollar.com and Richard's website boominglives.co.uk.)

My co-authors Bob Collie and Matthew X. Smith instantly gave me permission to use material we first published in *The Retirement Plan Solution*: thank you!

To Bill Chinery and his Cricket Club lunch gang (Malcolm Hamilton, John Ilkiw, Harold Nudelman, John Por, David Short, Bob Swan, Fred Vettese), my grateful thanks, not only for wonderful conversations on such a variety of topics, but for giving my life in Toronto some social stability when I moved back after 25 years away. And special thanks to Bill for his unfailing kindness, to Malcolm for being a role model as a professional, and to John P for keeping my professional life alive at a time when I might have let it fold.

The team at the Out:think Group (Joseph Hinson, Jael Sette and Nathan Torrence) created my website (https://donezra.com) and help maintain it in good working order. They held my hand through my virtual melt-down just before launching it, and I think of the analogy of stage plays, where the audience has no idea of all the things that cause panic backstage. Thank you!

Setaj Ladd (at Sage Studio) converted my vague notions into a series of pictorial metaphors from which I picked the ones for the book that I thought fitted best. My thanks for his imagination and skill!

Glendon Haddix (at Streetlight Graphics) spared me the anxious task of formatting the manuscript for publication – thanks for saving my sanity!

The notion of podcasts came from my friends at Common Wealth (Janette Luu, Alex Mazer, Jonathan Weisstub), who have carried most of the burden of creating them. Thank you!

I don't photograph well. Typically the result looks as if it's for a passport. So all the more credit and thanks to Sian Trenberth for getting me to look acceptable in more than one shot, so I actually had a choice. Wow!

REFERENCES

Aaker, Jennifer L., Melanie Rudd and Cassie Mogilner (2011). "If money does not make you happy, consider time" in the *Journal of Consumer Psychology* doi:10.1016/j.jcps.2011.01.004.

Anderson Elder Law (2015). "Planning with your adult children helps you remain in control," andersonelderlaw.com, March 24, 2015.

Ashford, Kate (2016). "New love: a retirement dream – or nightmare?" at www.bbc.com/capital/story/20160531-new-love-a-retirement-dream-or-nightmare (1 June 2016).

Bates, Larry (2018). *Beat the Bank: the Canadian Guide to Simply Successful Investing* (Audey Press).

Bernstein, William J. (2014). *If You Can: How Millennials Can Get Rich Slowly* (Efficient Frontier Publications).

Carstensen, Laura (2011). *A Long Bright Future: Happiness, Health and Financial Security in an Age of Increased Longevity* (Public Affairs, New York, NY).

Claxton, Guy (1997). *Hare Brain, Tortoise Mind: How Intelligence Increases When You Think Less* (Fourth Estate Limited).

Clements, Jonathan (2018). *From Here to Financial Happiness: Enrich Your Life in Just 77 Days* (Wiley).

Covey, Stephen R. (1989). *The 7 Habits of Highly Effective People* (Free Press/Simon & Schuster).

Crosby, Daniel, Ph.D. (2017). "Behavioral finance, with a focus on decumulation" at the IMCA Focus on Advanced Portfolio Construction Conference, Toronto, ON, September 18, 2017.

Dunn, Elizabeth W., Daniel T. Gilbert and Timothy D. Wilson (2011). "If money doesn't make you happy, then you probably aren't spending it right" in the *Journal of Consumer Psychology* doi:10.1016.j/jcps.2011.02.002.

Gilbert, Daniel T. (2006). *Stumbling on Happiness* (Knopf, New York, NY).

Hamilton, Malcolm (2015). "Do Canadians Save Too Little?" C.D. Howe Institute Commentary No. 428, June 2015.

Hogan, Michael, Ph.D. (2013). "Love at any age" by Michael Hogan Ph.D. at https://www.psychologytoday.com/blog/in-one-lifespan/201302/love-any-age.

Jacobson, Ed, Ph.D. (2011). "Re-energize and renew your relationships with high impact client review meetings" at the AICPA Advanced Personal Financial Planning Conference, Las Vegas, NV, January 10, 2011.

Kalish, Nancy, Ph.D. (2011). "Late-life remarriages: the second (or third...) time around" at https://www.psychologytoday.com/blog/sticky-bonds/201111/late-life-remarriages-the-second-or-third-time-around.

Kinder, George (2000). *The Seven Stages of Money Maturity* (Dell, New York, NY).

Levinson, Harry (1976). *Psychological Man* (Levinson Institute, Cambridge, MA).

MacDonald, Bonnie-Jeanne, Lars Osberg and Kevin D. Moore (2016). "How accurately does 70% final employment earnings replacement measure retirement income (in)adequacy? Introducing the Living Standards Replacement Rate (LSRR)" in ASTIN Bulletin, the *Journal of the IAA*, Vol. 46 Issue 3, September 2016.

Melone, Linda (2016). "Why couples divorce after decades of marriage: the 5 reasons for 'gray divorce' and what to do before it's too late" by Linda Melone, March 8, 2016, www.nextavenue.org.

Smith, Melinda, M.A. and Jeanne Segal, Ph.D. (2016). "Caregiving support and help: tips for making family caregiving easier and more rewarding" at www.helpguide.org, June 2016.

Sullivan, Paul (2016). "When dividing assets, the little things matter," *The New York Times*, April 15, 2016, http://nyti.ms/1quh16N.

Vettese, Frederick (2015). *The Essential Retirement Guide: A Contrarian's Perspective* (Wiley, 2015).

World Bank (1994). "Averting the old age crisis: policies to protect the old and promote growth." 1994. Washington DC: World Bank.

Zelinski, Ernie J. (2009). *How to Retire Happy, Wild and Free: Retirement Wisdom That You Won't Get from Your Financial Adviser* (VIP Books).